GREGOR EWING has a passion for the o
his interest in history. His first book,
his 500 mile walk in 2012 – accomp
following the route of Bonnie Prince Charlie's flight after the Bàttle
of Culloden. In 2014, he walked over 1,000 miles in a continuous
journey following in the footsteps of Robert the Bruce. *Bruce, Meg
and Me* is the story of the expedition. Gregor has given talks at literary,
history and outdoor festivals throughout Scotland and has spoken at
events organised by the National Library of Scotland and Culloden
Battlefield Centre. He lives in Falkirk with his wife, Nicola, and three
daughters, Sophie, Kara and Abbie. The dogs, Meg and Ailsa, complete
the female entourage in his household.

Bruce, Meg and Me

*An adventurous 1,000 mile walk
following Robert the Bruce as he struggled
to save Scotland*

GREGOR EWING

Luath Press Limited

EDINBURGH

www.luath.co.uk

First published 2015

ISBN: 978-1-910021-80-4

The author's right to be identified as author of this book
under the Copyright, Designs and Patents Act 1988 has been asserted.

The paper used in this book is recyclable. It is made
from low chlorine pulps produced in a low energy,
low emission manner from renewable forests.

Maps © Gregor Ewing. Base map information supplied
by Open Street & Cycle maps (and) contributors
(www.openstreetmap.org) and reproduced under the
Creative Commons Licence.

Printed and bound by The Charlesworth Group, Wakefield

Typeset in 10.5 point Sabon

Contents

List of Maps

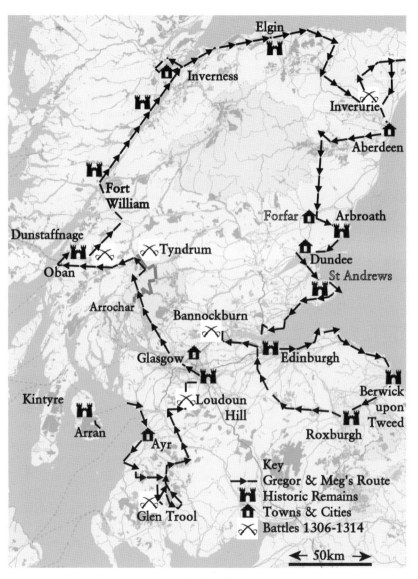

The Complete Journey.

To Nicola, Sophie, Kara and Abbie

Acknowledgements

It was only through the support of my wife Nicola that I was able to undertake my journey. A loving thanks to her for keeping the home fires burning.

Friends who met or accompanied on the way gave me great encouragement and helped keep me sane. Especially, George, Jennifer, Graeme and Iain.

Thanks to Andy Smith, Ian Scott and Jennie Renton at Luath who all helped turn my manuscript into the book in front of you today.

Once again I am grateful to Dr Tony Pollard, for finding time in his busy schedule to write a thoughtful and amusing foreword.

Foreword

SAY THE NAME Robert the Bruce and the next word that comes to mind is very likely Bannockburn. And even now, after years of studying the Scottish Wars of Independence and visiting their many battlefields it is still Bannockburn that I most strongly associate with him, despite the fact that his life story, and his military experience, consisted of so much more. I can perhaps be forgiven for this single-mindedness though, as the Battle of Bannockburn has probably taken up more of my time as a battlefield archaeologist than any other, from my first failure to find evidence for the battle site while making the television series *Two Men in a Trench* back in 2003, to finally being able to say with confidence where it was fought after an ambitious project in 2013–14.

It was the 700th anniversary of the Battle of Bannockburn in 2014 that really brought Robert the Bruce alive for many people and it was certainly the motivation for that successful project and the associated BBC TV programmes, *The Quest for Bannockburn,* presented by my old friend Neil Oliver and myself. One of the great pleasures of that project was the involvement of locals and school children in the quest; it was a real community undertaking, in which well over 1,000 volunteers took part. There were also other events to mark the occasion, which just happened to coincide closely with the Referendum for Scottish Independence (which failed to emulate Bruce's achievements), such as the opening of the new state-of-the-art visitor centre and the re-enactment of the battle at the *Bannockburn Live* weekend organised by the National Trust for Scotland.

But away from the crowds and the TV screens, a more personal and far more demanding tribute to the great man was taking place. Over the best part of two months in early 2014, Gregor Ewing and his faithful dog, Meg, undertook an epic walk of 1,000 miles as they followed the route of Robert the Bruce's movements through Scotland prior to the Battle of Bannockburn in June 1314. This was not the first time they had hiked back into history, in 2012 the pair followed the trail of Bonnie Prince Charlie from his defeat at Culloden in April

1746 to his rescue by a French ship off the west coast of Scotland the following August (a mere 530-mile stroll).

The idea of discovering and communicating history through the medium of a journey has always appealed to me. As a schoolboy, I hatched a scheme to follow the 1,170 mile route taken by the Nez Percé Indians under Chief Joseph from their reservation to freedom in Canada in 1877, all the way pursued by the US Army. Despite putting up some impressive fights they didn't make it. My plan, which I spent many an hour pondering, was to follow the route on the back of one of the Appaloosa ponies for which the tribe were well known. But alas, a daydream it remained. What's so impressive about Gregor is that he turns his daydreams into reality.

Back in 2014, while I roamed the carse fields adjacent to the banks of the Bannockburn, monitoring the progress of metal-detecting teams or keeping an eye on our volunteer archaeologists, so Gregor and Meg progressed from one corner of the country to the next, moving from one Bruce milestone to another. But as he documents here, at one point prior to setting out on his expedition he found time to take part in that project, digging one of our many test pits and to his delight finding a sherd of medieval pottery in it.

The journey has long been a metaphor for the human experience, albeit one that has recently strayed into saccharin cliché when it comes to the sort of challenges pursued on TV talent shows and dance competitions. In this book, however, Gregor reminds us that some of the most important periods of our history are made up of journeys, with momentous events such as powerful marriages, coronations and battles punctuating voyages, marches and expeditions, which in the days before motorised transport required considerable amounts of determination and stamina, and as Gregor found out, a hefty chunk of time.

Bruce was determined to be king of Scotland, to be the winner of what became known as the Great Cause, even if it meant committing murder, seeing his family almost wiped out, waging war and laying waste to large tracts of his own country. Travelling around the kingdom was an essential part of that process. In the days before mass communication it was essential that a monarch was seen by his people (seeing is after all believing), and Bruce was a graduate of the 'if you want something done well, do it yourself' school. It is said that even the appearance of an unwell Bruce, who at that point was carried on a litter, was enough to send his enemies fleeing the field at Inverurie in 1308. In any case, his army was never really big enough to send men off on one campaign while he fought another – an exception was the Irish campaign of 1315–18 and that ended in disaster (see below). So it was that he spent much of his life marching from one place to another, exterminating his enemies, impressing his allies and awing his people.

Winning the crown was hard work, and even though victory at Bannockburn was to establish him as king in Scotland, there was a long way to go before England would accept the independence of their northern neighbour (the Scottish Wars of Independence did not come to an end until 1355). It's a fact that even now, after the 700th anniversary, many people don't realise that Bannockburn did not end the story, but as Gregor's book so ably demonstrates, there was also lot going in Bruce's life before the most famous battle in Scotland's history was fought.

Gregor has provided an entertaining account of a journey made by man and dog, which also weaves in the story of key incidents in Bruce's life as he made his own progressions around Scotland over 700 years ago. Away from Bannockburn my work, in this case on the compilation of Historic Scotland's Inventory of Historic Battlefields, has taken me to the sites of other key battles fought by Bruce, including the Methven, Loudon Hill and Inverurie. I have even followed the trail, by car I hasten to add, of his brother's ill-fated campaign in Ireland, which took place between 1315 and 1318 and ended with Edward Bruce's death at the Battle of Foughart. As a demonstration that seeing was believing it is not too much of a digression to point out that Edward's head was sent to Edward II and his limbs dispatched to all the corners of Ireland, all to prove that he was in fact dead. This series of special deliveries also demonstrates that death need not be a barrier to travel back in Bruce's day.

Despite my own encounters with the landscapes of Robert Bruce,

I am not ashamed to admit that there are battlefields that Gregor and Meg visited which I have not. These include Glen Trool, where Bruce demonstrated a talent for Guerrilla warfare when he ambushed a larger mounted English force. There are also in these pages a number of stories I had not come across before, and as a battlefield archaeologist found most tantalising. One of these relates to farmers digging up weapons from their fields before Clatteringshaws Loch was created as a reservoir. I was also as surprised as Gregor to learn that St Conan's Kirk on the banks of Loch Awe contains one of Bruce's toe bones. I have driven past that church on numerous occasions, and if I had known would definitely have stopped off to pay my respects.

I cannot end without making a small confession. It was not difficult to say yes to penning this Foreword to the book when Gregor invited me to do so, way back before he had started his journey. I was interested in the subject matter and confident it would be good, as he had more than proven his abilities as an engaging writer with *Charlie, Meg and Me*, for which I had been pleased to provide the same service (though back then he was an unknown quantity). Good intentions are not the same as fulfilled promises, though, and so it was that I found myself buried in other writing tasks when Gregor very politely asked via email whether I had read the manuscript and therefore made any progress with the foreword; he did after all have a publication schedule. To my shame I had not even begun to read it, despite it being in my possession for some time by then, such had been the distraction of my other projects. Ah well, I thought, it's Friday and I'll give it a quick skim-read before dashing something off and getting back to him on Monday. I am being so candid here because the best recommendation I can make for this book is that my intention to read a section here and a section there, just enough to allow me to fulfil my promise, came to nought as it proved to be such a page turner that I didn't put it down before having read it from cover to cover.

Where will Gregor's next epic walk take him? Well, at one point in these pages he makes a passing remark about wanting to drive cattle along ancient drove roads from the Western Isles to the cattle market at Falkirk. It just so happens that I spent some time living next to an old drove road near Oban as a child and the idea of driving cattle over a long distance has always appealed. After all, what self-respecting man of my age didn't want to be a cowboy in his callow youth? I suspect also that, if relieved of her backpack, Meg would make a splendid cattle dog. Accordingly, I have told Greg that no such undertaking is to be made without me. It might, however, be some time before you see *Tony, Meg, the Coos and Me*, on the shelves of your local bookshop.

Tony Pollard,
Glasgow, March 2015

Introduction

IN 2012, I fulfilled a long held desire to escape to the hills. In a continuous journey, I walked over 850km (530 miles), following the route of Bonnie Prince Charlie's escape after the disastrous Battle of Culloden in 1746. Carrying my own food, shelter and equipment, and with just my border collie, Meg, for company I retraced the Prince's route through the Highlands and Islands of northwest Scotland. Returning to the comforts of home, I wrote up my adventures, and was delighted to get *Charlie, Meg and Me* published. I did a short promotional book tour and was regularly asked, 'What's your next escapade?'

Following Bonnie Prince Charlie's escape had been one of the highlights of my life, which I imagined would be a one-off. But hey, why not? Once the seed was sewn it didn't take me long to decide to attempt something similar and I realised that with the 700th anniversary of the Battle of Bannockburn approaching, surely it was a perfect time to follow the struggles of Robert the Bruce. The story was captivating, took in large swathes of Scotland and was of particular personal interest to me: Nigel Tranter's *Bruce Trilogy* had been the spark which flamed my lifelong interest in Scotland's history. Undoubtedly though, the seminal book was GWS Barrow's *Robert Bruce and the Community of the Realm of Scotland*, which I consulted to see if it would be feasible to follow in Bruce's footsteps.

The Battle of Bannockburn, Scotland's most famous military victory, was masterminded by Robert the Bruce, who went on to restore the country's status as an independent kingdom in the 14th century. The story I wanted to tell was that of the early years of Bruce's kingship, when tearing Scotland back from the clutches of England's Plantagenet rulers looked beyond the realms of serious possibility.

Within five months of being crowned King of Scots in 1306 by a small band of supporters, Bruce was defeated three times in battle and forced into hiding on the myriad of islands off Scotland's rugged west coast. The following year, on his return to the mainland at Turnberry, he overcame tremendous adversity to establish his kingship, unite the country and inflict defeat upon a nation, far larger and more powerful, than his own. This transformation of fortunes is what Barrow calls 'one of the great heroic enterprises of History'.

For my own part, I wanted to push my own boundaries and go further than my previous walk. Seven hundred miles on the 700th anniversary of Bruce's great triumph seemed both appropriate and achievable. I also wanted to follow as accurately as I could Bruce's return to Scotland in 1307 when he began the attempt to win back his crown. This campaign of 1307-08, a civil war, laid the foundations for (although it by no means guaranteed) future success. Thereafter, Robert focused on defeating the occupying forces of Edward II and pressurising him to recognise Scotland as an independent realm. I soon realised that I couldn't fit all this history into 700 miles (1100km) and the distance crept up towards 1,000 miles (1,600km) which my ego embraced before my legs could put in an appeal. I ended up with a route which would allow me to follow Bruce from his lowest ebb to ultimate triumph. The main part of this journey would take me round Scotland in a clockwise direction, starting in Galloway, travelling northward, through Argyll and up the Great Glen to Inverness. After crossing over to the Black Isle, I would return to Moray and Aberdeenshire before continuing south, down the east coast, all the way to the border with England and the town of Berwick upon Tweed. Turning around I would march back through the hills to the Forth Valley and Bannockburn. Following the King's route wherever possible, and when this was unknown, Scotland's Great Trails (West Highland Way, Great Glen Way, etc) would be tramped upon between the historic locations.

Accompanied by my dog, Meg, we would be carrying our own food and equipment. I aimed to cover about 30km (19 miles) per day and would wild camp most evenings – only occasionally would I take advantage of the facilities of a campsite.

Over the course of 12 months I researched the history in detail in order to get to know the story intimately. I wanted to arrive at a castle, monument or battlefield knowing the background. There wouldn't be time to learn the story as I went, but I hoped to add to my knowledge at each place I visited. Poring over my collection of maps was enjoyable as I sought to find a suitable and accurate route that would keep me in the countryside as much as possible. In between my day job, the research, and the planning, I went running four times a week to build up my fitness once more – the physical prowess gained from my previous walk had been lost completely when I gave up all exercise to concentrate on writing my first book. During that time, too often did I find myself during blank moments staring into the fridge seeking inspiration. For a whole year Meg had been dozing under the kitchen table dreaming of her previous adventures – walking round the block just wasn't the same anymore. I was excited for her as well as for myself as the day drew near.

Considering my three school-age kids and a very understanding wife would have to cope without me for a lengthy period of absence, it behoved me to make this a worthwhile journey. I was determined to uncover something new about the legendary Bruce, to help justify my, let's face it, selfish retreat from the responsibilities of everyday life. With my bag packed, my body in half-decent shape and my route planned out in detail, I was ready for the off. Then I got a phone call!

Gregor Ewing,
Falkirk, May 2015

Historical Prologue

THE SCOTTISH WARS of Independence and the subsequent rise of Robert the Bruce came about after King Alexander III of Scotland died in 1286, leaving only an infant in distant Norway as heir to the throne. Scotland and England had evolved from the Dark Ages into the medieval period as separate realms, the last two on an island that once held many small kingdoms. There had been peace between the two countries for 30 years, during which time Scotland had flourished: Alexander's reign was looked back on by later chroniclers as a golden period in Scotland's story.

The Maid of Norway, as the child became known, died en route to Scotland, and in order to prevent a bloody civil war, King Edward, a respected neighbour, was asked by the Scots nobility and clergy to choose a new king for their country. A number of claimants came forward, including a certain Robert Bruce, grandfather of the future King Robert I. However, Edward deemed Robert Bruce's claim to be inferior to that of John Balliol, who was duly selected as King of Scots in 1292.

In accepting the crown, John Balliol paid homage to Edward I as his feudal superior, making the Scottish King subordinate to his English counterpart. This situation lasted for four years, with Edward making increasing demands upon John until eventually the Scottish King rebelled, culminating in the Battle of Dunbar in 1296. The Scottish army was defeated; John was stripped of his crown (as well as the embroidered lions off his coat) and sent to the Tower of London.

Edward decided to rule Scotland directly – royal castles were garrisoned, sheriffs appointed to collect taxes and justiciars to administer English law in Scotland. Armed revolt was almost immediate and after defeating an English army at the Battle of Stirling Bridge in 1297, William Wallace was appointed Guardian of Scotland, acting in the name of the imprisoned King John.

Wallace's army was defeated at Falkirk the following year and he resigned from the position. Other guardians followed, including John

Comyn and Robert the Bruce himself. The Scots maintained a spirited resistance to Edward but by 1305 their defeat was complete. The people's patriot William Wallace was dead, and virtually all Scotsmen of senior rank had submitted to Edward. Scotland was incorporated within the land of England and would be ruled by a council appointed by the English King.

Then in February 1306, a crime was committed which even in such brutal and turbulent times must have caused shock waves. Robert the Bruce, whose family were strong contenders for the vacant throne in 1286, claimed the crown of Scotland for himself in the most dramatic fashion. He stabbed John Comyn, his main rival for the resumption of a Scottish kingship, in front of the high altar and within the sanctuary of Greyfriars Church in Dumfries, a shocking crime in the most sacred of places.

Within a few weeks, Bruce was crowned King of Scots at Scone in as authentic a ceremony as was possible given the short timespan. The Scottish Church forgave Bruce's crime for the sake of the nation and supported him. Amongst the attendees at the coronation were three bishops and four earls, the most senior magnates in the country.

Edward I was incensed by Bruce's uprising. Despite being known as 'Hammer of the Scots' after his death, Edward found in life that the nails just kept popping out. A special lieutenant, Aymer de Valence, was despatched to Scotland, backed by an army holding aloft the dreaded dragon banner signalling that the rules by which warfare was conducted were suspended: there would be no mercy for anyone connected with Bruce's rising.

Robert's attempt to establish authority and control in Scotland was ended swiftly when he was comprehensively defeated at Methven, near Perth, in June 1306. Aymer de Valence sent his forces out on a night attack and caught Bruce's army by surprise. The King himself only just escaped; other prominent supporters were caught and executed. In the surviving sources, there are faint details of a second encounter on the banks of Loch Tay as the remnants of Bruce's army were pursued by the victors.[1]

The new king remained at large, but he was ambushed along with his last remaining forces at Strath Fillan by a force of Highlanders under the command of John MacDougall, loyal to the Comyn family and now in allegiance with Edward I.

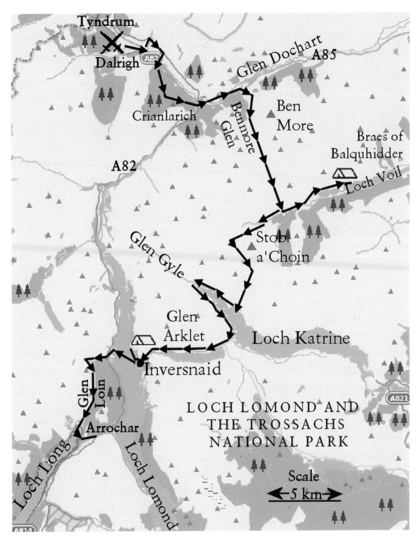

Loch Lomond and the Trossachs National Park.

CHAPTER I

The Trossachs and Arran

FROM THE OUTSET, I had planned to begin my journey on Rathlin Island, just off the coast of Northern Ireland. After his defeat at Dalrigh, the King was forced to flee Scotland and he spent some time on this small island during the winter of 1306–07 before returning to begin the attempt to reclaim his kingdom. Rathlin seemed like the perfect place from which to launch my own invasion. In some D-Day-like dream, I had envisaged Meg and myself standing on the prow of a small craft, watching Scotland's shoreline gradually fill the horizon. Approaching the beach, battered only by the wind and rain, we would jump into the sea and run onto the soft white sand of the Kintyre peninsula. Unfortunately, just a few days before the start of my trip, the captain of the private charter boat I had hired, called to say that upcoming bad weather in the Irish Sea was going to make the sailing impossible. I couldn't delay the trip as I had various rendezvous planned later in the walk, so I had no option but to cancel this leg of the journey. Instead, I made some hasty plans and headed towards Tyndrum in the Trossachs.

So instead of a dreamy sojourn to a mysterious island, I began my journey at Dalrigh, just to the south of Tyndrum. On a bright, sunny day, this is a beautiful Highland landscape, with mountains, glens and rivers begging exploration. On a dull, wet and windy March morning, with the clouds just above head-height, it was just foreboding. My father-in-law dropped me off. After a short stroll together, a quick cheerio to him was far easier than my parting from home early that morning when everyone was upset, not least my wife as she contemplated nine weeks of juggling her full-time job, looking after the house and ferrying the children around, all on her lonesome.

The idea behind this hastily cobbled-together start to my journey was to follow the escape of King Robert the Bruce after he was defeated in battle for the third time in quick succession. This was a disastrous start to his revival of a kingship that had lain dormant since the forced abdication of King John Balliol ten years earlier. It was July 1306, Bruce had been King of Scots for less than four months, and it looked like his reign was to be the briefest of all Scottish monarchs. After reverses at Methven and Loch Tay, the remnants of his army crossed the River Fillan at Dalrigh where they were ambushed by a force of Highlanders under the command of John MacDougall.

There are no detailed descriptions of the battle, but as I stood by the ford I could easily imagine an army of screaming, leaping clansmen emerging from the mist. Bruce's ragtag forces, caught unawares, would have been seriously handicapped. They were caught in the midst of an awkward manoeuvre and burdened by the injured as well as by the women and children of the new royal family. MacDougall's lightly armed Highlanders would have been at a distinct advantage on the rough ground and the mounted men of Bruce's party would have been unable to deploy properly. An inscribed stone bench, between the river and Dalrigh field, marks the spot where Robert and his followers were ambushed. Retreating, they passed little Lochan nan Arm on the south side of the River Fillan, where the King and his followers discarded some of their weapons. At some point during this retreat, the King split up his party and sent his Queen and other prominent females away under the guidance and protection of his brother Nigel. With just a few men left, Bruce took to the hills to make his escape. The King of Scots was now a powerless fugitive in his own country, his army defeated and many of his supporters captured or slain. Powerful and numerous enemies were bent on destroying him, and he was far from friendly territory where he could find safety.

I started walking in the direction of Bruce's retreat. Meg trotted beside me, knowing full well something major was beginning, because she had been saddled with a cumbersome rucksack. Local legend informs us that King Robert was forced to fight a running battle south-wards and I followed the river down Strath Fillan on the footpath of the West Highland Way, the oldest and best known of Scotland's Great Trails.[2] Crossing under the A85 and with the tiniest of diversions I was

The River Fillan; on the far side, the field of Dalrigh.

soon at a natural widening of the river, looking at the Holy Pool of St Fillan. In bygone days, those with mental ailments went for a dip in the healing waters. Had I gone for a swim, then suitably cured I'd have been back in the car with my father-in-law. A 1,000 mile continuous walk! Only a dog for company and 65 nights in a tent in Scotland! Madness!

The West Highland Way runs through Auchtertyre Farm and then past the scanty remains of a once substantial St Fillan's Priory. This Augustinian priory was once over 50m in length and it was endowed by Bruce 11 years after his defeat here in 1306. St Fillan himself was an 8th-century monk who preached in this area. His sacred relics were revered and looked after by the Dewars of the Coigreach – the crozier and bell belonging to St Fillan survive to this day. In 1306, having already received forgiveness for his murder of John Comyn from the dominant Roman Church, Bruce was quite possibly in this area seeking forgiveness from the Celtic Church in the presence of these holy relics. The relics were called into use prior to the Battle of Bannockburn in 1314.

Most walkers tackle the West Highland Way from Milngavie to Fort William, the scenery becoming more dramatic as they head towards the Highlands. I was going against the flow of walkers on this short stretch, and I was determined to make the effort to talk to as many people as possible during my walk, hopefully picking up little bits of advice or local knowledge as well as exercising underused vocal chords. I tried a few introductory lines like 'Where are you heading?' or 'Have you come far?' but just as 'Do you come here often?' never seemed to work for me on the dance floor, I didn't get much response. Letting Meg do the talking seemed to work better as she immediately gained sympathy for her friendly demeanour and cruel panniers.

Crossing the main road again, the path heads uphill through a dense forestry plantation before descending to Crianlarich at the southern end of Strath Fillan. Passing through this village of converging routes, surrounded on all sides by 1,000m mountains, I followed a disused railway track alongside the A85 before coming to Loch Dochart. On a small island in the centre of the loch, partially hidden by trees, was a 16th-century castle. Unfortunately, 19th-century repairs made the ruins resemble an industrial chimney and spoiled the scene.

Under the shadow of Ben More, the conical shape of which is so recognisable from Scotland's Central Belt and which issues a magnetic charm to many Lowland walkers, I followed a track past a farm at the foot of the hill and continued on into Benmore Glen. Getting wetter and colder as I climbed gradually southwards, a sense of impending doom began to creep over me. Reaching a bealach (mountain pass) at a height of 500m, there were snow fields on the slopes above and patches of ice underfoot. A crisis of confidence, mixed with a little bit of guilt, engulfed me. Why the hell was I doing this? What was I thinking about, spending weeks and weeks outdoors again? It had been two years since my previous foray into the hills and I had forgotten how cold, wet and lonely it could be. The rucksack felt bloody heavy as well; I couldn't imagine day after day with this on my back. How selfish was I, leaving my family behind for over nine weeks to go on some self-fulfilling odyssey?

Trying to banish this negativity from my overactive mind, I tried to latch onto something positive, something to look forward to – but there were no cosy B&B's on this trip; no meeting with friends or family for a while yet; no little carrots to dangle in front of my mind's eye.

Plodding on morosely, I reached the summit of the flattened,

The Braes of Balquhidder, Loch Doine and, in the distance, Loch Voil.

boulder-strewn pass separating the misty mountains of Stob Binnein and Cruach Ardrain. Descending south by the tumbling white waters of the Inverlochlarig Burn, which was bulging with snow melt, a track appeared and took me down to the Glen of Balquhidder, where Bruce is reputed to have retreated to after the battle.[3] Still feeling low, I took advantage of a dry spell to stop for an early dinner and took shelter within a little piece of community woodland which gave me some protection from the bitterly cold wind. Dried pasta and instant custard was certainly no gourmet meal, but I devoured it. Thereafter, with a full belly and a mug of scorching hot black coffee in hand, my spirits were fortified.

Heading east along the glen, I reached the smaller of two lochs beautifully set in a narrow valley overlooked by steep-sided hills – the Braes of Balquhidder. Loch Doine connects with Loch Voil, at the head of which was my destination, 'Bruce's Stone', where Robert is said to have rested, having finally having fought off the last of the pursuers from the battle. It must have been a long chase; I had walked 26km to get to this point, having fought only my own inner turmoil, and yet I was still shattered.

The large, oblong stone with a Scots pine sprouting forth atop was situated in a small cove and surrounded by dark, lapping waters.

Bruce's stone surrounded by the raised waters of Loch Voil.

The most prominent clans in the area, Fergusons, MacLarens and MacGregors, all claim to have helped Bruce here in the Braes of Balquhidder and led him to a cave in the nearby cliffs, where he took shelter for the night.[4] As I was walking along the road by the lochside, a Land Rover pulled up and the driver offered me a lift. I sought, instead, help in finding this shelter. Having spent his childhood in the glen, the fella knew of the cave I was looking for, but warned it was hard to find – and that it was more of a rock overhang than a cave, over which water poured during wet spells.

Disheartened, I trudged up the hillside in the gathering dusk, lacking any belief that I could find this place – anyway, I told myself, it sounded like a rotten place to spend the night. A decision on whether or not to sleep in the cave wasn't needed, because in the woods at the foot of the brae I lost a walking pole which had been slipped through a belt loop on my trousers. When I eventually noticed its disappearance, my weakened mental state gave way to self-recrimination – it took 20 minutes of frantic searching before I stumbled upon it, and my efforts brought a momentary surge of delight before fading light gave me a good excuse to stop for the day. Thoroughly exhausted, I pitched my tent almost where I stood: on a slope in the forest, in the rain.

Lying in the tent, squeezed alongside Meg and the bulbous rucksack, I was thoroughly miserable at the thought of what I had let myself in for. I regretted my living-room adventurousness, and the rashness with which I had upped the total length of the walk to 1,000 miles (1,600km). On top of all that, my hastily arranged start had added another three days' hard walking, rather than the relaxing sail which should have been my introduction. How was I going to cope in a cramped tent in the rain, night after night? I was feeling claustrophobic, deflated and exhausted after just one day. Tomorrow's itinerary looked worse and I had blisters already (partly due to the purchase of light trail shoes which had gotten soaked through in minutes, and moved around my feet so much more than well-fitting boots). It was only mid-March, the weather could be wet for weeks yet, and cold nights were guaranteed. Why wasn't I at home with my family, reading my youngest daughter a bedtime story? Hot cocoa waiting. Suddenly the humdrum routine of everyday life seemed ever so enticing. For Pete's sake, I was past 40. Give me my pipe and slippers!

Even in the shelter of the woods it was a rough night, with the whistling wind, heavy rain and disturbing dreams. The weather was still grim in the morning so I packed up on an empty stomach and moved on. No point in searching for the cave now: that ship had sailed. Local legend has it that Bruce left the fragments of his broken sword at the cave. While resting there, it seems the King had better dreams than me, he had a vision of an 'old man with grey locks who foretold his future destiny'.[5]

My aim was to reach Inversnaid, where there was the appeal of locating yet another cave in which the King of Scots took shelter. There was also a ferry (weather dependent – it had been cancelled in the days prior to my departure, due to high water levels) that would take me across Loch Lomond towards the Clyde Estuary, my destination.

Retracing my steps of the previous evening, I headed west, back along the lochside road. Soon I was passing the Monachyle Mhor Hotel and in a moment of weakness I decided to check it out. This luxury establishment was washed in pink – at one time this bright finish would have signalled that the owner was a Jacobite. Encouraged somewhat by this signal, Meg and I skulked up the gravel drive in full view of the residents breakfasting in the glass conservatory. As we approached, the entrance doors were thrown open and a confident individual came striding out and warmly welcomed us in. Walking with a huge rucksack and a wet dog, I am never sure of the reception that I'll receive at fancy establishments, so it was nice to be made to feel wanted from the outset. Inside the hotel, I retreated to a cosy bar and after shedding some wet layers I plonked myself down and relaxed. The tension in mind and body lifted almost immediately in the comforting surroundings and I splashed out and ordered a full Scottish breakfast. It was 9am and reasonably busy; the comings and goings of the guests and staff were a welcome distraction from thoughts of my walk. While I was waiting to be fed, the waiter rushed into the bar and removed a smoke detector. I assumed my breakfast had been delayed, or worse, cremated. As the burning smell started to travel, the guy who had welcomed me stormed into the kitchen, and screamed, 'What have you done?' I listened intently for the next sound, surely frying pan onto bone. However, there was only a meek squeak from the kitchen and I knew there was humour, not fury, in the boss's rant; I smiled from ear to ear.

Loath as I was to leave this establishment, at least I was cheered up, filled up and dried up by the time I dragged myself away. Back on the road I met Peter, a retired Dutch Marine, out walking his dog; he worked on the estate, so I speired him for a bit of local knowledge about the going up ahead.

At the end of the public road, I walked past Inverlochlarig farm and onto a track before crossing a bridge over the River Larig. Blocking access to the hillside was a fence built in a strong defensive position; almost, but not quite invulnerable to attack by a man encumbered by a heavy rucksack. Only by using superior and previously unknown gymnastic skills did I manage to progress (a lift and drop technique was practised on the dog). Now in open country, negotiating a river of streams cascading off the hillside, I made my way round a shoulder of Stob a'Choin, my clothes and footwear as sodden as the ground. The rain continued as I slogged uphill on the west side of the mountain. Breathless, I reached a long, level, mushy pass encapsulating a little lochan which fed the Allt a Choin. I followed this deeply cutting river as it worked its way southwards and as I descended towards Loch Katrine it became an ever more mesmerising and raging torrent. Thankfully, as it approached feeding time again, the rain relented and the clouds parted a little. Under an upliftingly bright sky, I seized my opportunity and tied my sodden tent and waterproofs to a fence, then cooked up some egg noodles whilst my washing billowed in the wind.

Beautiful Loch Katrine, at the heart of the Trossachs, has been a destination for sightseers ever since Queen Victoria sailed up the loch in 1866. The steamship ss *Sir Walter Scott* has been working the waters for over a century. Don't bring your speedboat, though; oil-fired engines are banned – you wouldn't want to come between Glaswegians and their water supply. I reached the private road that borders the loch and in front of me was a man-made peninsula extending into the water, at the end of which was an 18th-century Clan MacGregor burial ground – a stunning location to spend eternity.

Marching along the road, I passed the head of the loch at Glengyle, where the most famous MacGregor of them all, Rob Roy, was born. A lady approached from a distance with two dogs and I watched her put them on leads. Meg and I passed without incident so I turned

The cave reputedly used by both Robert the Bruce and Rob Roy.

and stopped for a chat. She informed me of a new footpath from Stronachlachar to Inversnaid. Then, without warning, one of her dogs exploded with anger and had a right good go at Meg, snapping, biting and nearly pulling the woman off her feet. Luckily for Meg, her rucksack took the brunt of the attack. After getting the dog under control, the woman explained that these were rescue dogs, and she had been warned that this dog didn't like other canines. I admired her courage in providing a home for an aggressive dog; it certainly forced her to find remote places to walk. But really, with a pet like that, how could she relax and enjoy the outdoors. It was a heck of a personal sacrifice. Meg seemed none the worse physically, although it couldn't have done her confidence any good.

Sure enough, when I reached Stronachlachar there was indeed a brand new footpath and against a strong headwind I fought my way down Glen Arklet. My emotions were stabilising a bit. I relaxed, let go of the lead and let my mind wander.

From the hamlet of Inversnaid it was just a last agonising kilometre on my tortured feet downhill to the Inversnaid Hotel, which was built in 1790 on the banks of Loch Lomond. I considered wimping out and getting a room rather than seeking out Bruce's cave, but when I arrived at the large, plush hotel, dogs weren't allowed inside; so, that was that! On a positive note, I discovered the ferry service across to Inveruglas was running again, saving me a long walk round the loch.

The cave just to the north of the Inversnaid Hotel was reputedly used by both Rob Roy and Robert the Bruce during their various predicaments. Bruce took shelter here and he crossed Loch Lomond near to this point. Formed by a tumble of boulders, the cave was easy enough to find but a bit of a scramble to reach. From the West Highland Way a sign directs and, very helpfully, 'CAVE' is painted in white letters on the rock face next to the entrance. From its elevated position, there are excellent views across the loch, giving any occupants fair warning of enemies approaching from the far bank. Climbing through the small triangular entrance hole, I squeezed onto a ledge below which there was a larger flat area of shelter lit by a gap between the boulders. When Bruce sat here, he was a tired and hungry fugitive;

undoubtedly he was also feeling completely dejected at the collapse of his fortunes. He couldn't have known, nor could he have imagined, that things were to get a lot worse before they got better.

Although the interior is large enough to accommodate six huddled people at a push, I didn't fancy it. The rock was wet and puddles congregated on the flat surfaces. I was too tired and not mentally strong enough yet to cope with a sleepless night in a dripping cave. Instead, I set up my tent at a small inlet by the shore of the loch. It had been another long day of around 30km, but I felt much more positive than I had the previous evening.

In the morning, Meg and I crossed Loch Lomond on the passenger ferry belonging to the hotel. As usual, Meg broke the ice with people we met, very few having seen a dog carrying a rucksack, so she was a bit of a cuddly curiosity. Each time I explained my proposed walk to someone, it hardened the glue that was holding me together. Bruce crossed Loch Lomond at a similar point. With his handpicked group crossing three at a time in a leaky rowing boat, they remained undetected as their pursuers searched in vain for them.

Landing at Inveruglas, I crossed the main road and followed the Loch Sloy footpath, one of the main access points for the surrounding mountains, the 'Arrochar Alps'. As Ben Vane loomed ahead I turned away southwards, and headed into Glen Loin, where a footpath runs the length of the valley between a break in the forestry plantation. At one time, the cattle reivers of Clan MacLaren ran up and down the glen. Now the only thing running along the glen were electricity pylons, which spoiled an otherwise nice section of walk. Upon reaching the village of Arrochar I had completed the preliminary stage of my walk, but mentally I was still struggling to cope and couldn't quite embrace my little achievement. Little did I realise the symmetry of the hastily planned start to my walk versus that of Bruce's own hasty, unplanned flight through the Trossachs.

The village of Arrochar sits at the head of Loch Long, which connects with the Firth of Clyde. In August 1306, having avoided his pursuers, Bruce sailed down the Firth of Clyde in a boat belonging to his supporter the Earl of Lennox. Bruce probably sailed down the Clyde from the Dumbarton area a good bit further to the south. Arrochar was the best I could manage with my three-day window of opportunity after the cancellation of the original start to my trip.

Bruce sailed past the Isle of Bute, stopping at Saddell Abbey on the Kintyre Peninsula before continuing onwards to Dunaverty Castle on the very tip of the long finger of land. Entrusting himself to Angus Og of the Isles, the King of Scots was spirited away. Only a few days later, English soldiers arrived and set siege to the castle, believing that Bruce was still within.

Where Robert the Bruce went that winter of 1306–07 may never be properly established. Much of what we do know of Bruce's life comes from the work of John Barbour, Archdeacon of Aberdeen, whose poem *The Bruce* was written around 1375. It is a masterpiece of Scottish literature and an important account of the history of Robert the Bruce.[5]

Barbour writes that Bruce sailed to Rathlin, an island off the coast of Northern Ireland. On Rathlin there is both a sea cave and a ruinous castle named after the King. However, it is a small island in which Bruce may have found himself trapped, had word of his stay reached his enemies. Nor would he have had the opportunity to find enough new recruits here, so he surely moved on. Another chronicler, John of Fordun, also writing in the late 14th century, has Bruce receiving support from Christian (MacRuari) of the Isles, who was a major power in the West Highlands and Islands. One of her residences, part of her Lordship of Garmoran, was the stunning Castle Tioram on the western seaboard at Moidart. Modern-day historian GWS Barrow, whose acclaimed book on Robert the Bruce was the source of much of my journey planning,[6] suggests that the King's recruiting was done not only in the islands off the west coast of Scotland, but also northern Ireland. In 1307, backed by these recruits, Bruce made his return to the Scottish mainland via the Isle of Arran, which was where I would catch up with him once more, determined not to let him go until I reached Bannockburn nine weeks hence.

I walked through the woods towards Arrochar Rail Station, to begin my journey to Arran. The sign said 3.6km, whereas on my map it looked less than 2km. I galloped along the footpath as best I could, and arrived at the station breathless, and an hour early! In the waiting room, I primped both the dog and myself as we prepared to come into contact with regular people again. The journey to Glasgow, poring over maps in a warm carriage, passed in a flash and soon Meg and I were walking down Buchanan Street. In this busy shopping precinct, passing smartly dressed shoppers, I was completely out of place and only too aware of my unkempt appearance. I felt like a hobo, seeking sympathy with my cute dog; she drew warm smiles and I drew hard stares. At Central Station, I boarded a train bound for Ardrossan Harbour and relaxed. The final stage of the journey was a calm sail across the Firth of Clyde to Brodick. Sitting in the pet friendly section of the large ferry, I got talking to a lady and her daughter who lived on the island. Meg was the catalyst for a conversation and the lady explained how she gave up her job as a social worker in Newcastle to start a business and a new life on Arran. Her daughter, aged 14 at the time, was horrified at the prospect of leaving the city, but eventually agreed to give it a six-month trial. Fast forward five years: the young woman considers Arran her home, and although she is now studying at Glasgow University, she plans to live on the island in the future.

Upon arrival at Brodick, I walked along the main street and reneged on my plan not to use B&B's. There was just not enough enthusiasm in my bones to walk out of town and find a spot to camp in the dark. Unfortunately, after having found just about the only place that took dogs, someone, somehow, somewhere took revenge on me for wimping out. Settling down on a comfortable bed with a few cold snacks, ready to enjoy a bit of TV, I got sharp stomach cramps. My relaxing evening was ruined and it was a sleepless night, racing back and forth to the toilet. I forced myself up at breakfast time but couldn't eat anything; thoroughly miserable, I abandoned my plans for the day and went back to bed. In the afternoon I raised myself once more, wanting to achieve something. I attempted to walk along to Brodick Castle, just round the bay from the town. Even without a rucksack this short journey was a struggle and by the time I reached the castle my weakened body ached from head to foot.

Brodick Castle, sitting high above Brodick Bay, was developed and built upon over a period of 700 years; a large Victorian tower is now the most dominant and lofty feature. In the 14th century, the castle consisted of a large stone keep and an impressive circular tower. A curtain wall defended the courtyard, which contained timber buildings. An elongated barbican defended the gatehouse and a moat surrounded the landward side. Just like Bruce's men, I found the gatehouse barred. It was still low season and only open at weekends.

The turnaround in Bruce's fortunes began here, although the King himself did not participate. His soon to be famous lieutenant, James Douglas, commanded a small raiding force which attacked a party of English sailors supplying victuals to the castle garrison. The booty of arms, clothes and food would have been most welcome. A detachment from the castle sallied forth to help their comrades, but was defeated and the survivors were chased back from whence they had sprung. To add to English misery, an onshore wind prevented the supply boats from sailing out of the bay and these ships were also captured by the Scots.

I hobbled back towards the B&B, now with my back in spasms and my butt clenched tightly. Thoroughly depressed, I thought about jacking the whole thing in. Four days in and I was totally fed up. I called my wife, who was surprised and horrified by my mental state. Nicola reminded me that I had told anyone who would listen that I was going, and what about all the publicity that had marked my departure? This rousing of my vanity was the saving of me – the mental anguish, the runs and now the bloody back pains still didn't quite outweigh the shame and embarrassment of walking down Falkirk High Street and meeting someone I knew: 'Oh, hello Gregor, I thought you were away on your walk.'

CHAPTER 2

Turnberry and the Galloway Hills

THE MALAISE PASSED as quickly as it had arrived. By the next morning, my insides had firmed up, my back was much better and the sun was shining. Overjoyed that my body had returned to its normal condition, Meg and I got back on the bus, both physically and psychologically. The excited chatter of the school kids reconvening with friends on their way to high school at Lamlash matched my own feelings.

The day lost to illness cost me the chance to walk to the King's Cave near Blackwaterfoot on the west coast of Arran, one of the locations where Bruce is reputed to have taken shelter. Although the cave contains medieval graffiti, its location doesn't quite fit with what we know of Bruce's movements. During his escape, he sailed down the Kintyre Peninsula and when Bruce reappears in the history books, following his mysterious winter, it was here on the east coast of Arran.

From the main road I walked with a fresh zing in my step down to Kingscross Point. An old circular fort sits at this promontory, guarding the southern entrance to Lamlash Bay, one of the best natural harbours

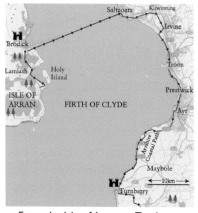

From the Isle of Arran to Turnberry.

in Britain. In 1263, King Hakon of Norway gathered his ships in the bay to invade Scotland. Forty-three years later, Robert the Bruce did the same, awaiting a sign from the mainland telling him that conditions were favourable to cross the Firth of Clyde. Beside the fort there is a cairn that supports a small standing stone. Although possibly dating to the Bronze Age, local tradition says that the stone was placed here to commemorate

From the Iron Age fort at Kingscross Point, Arran, looking over to Holy Island.

Bruce's departure. Holy Island, currently a Buddhist retreat, lies across the bay. The central peak on the island, Mullach Mor, would have made an ideal vantage point to look out for a signal fire at Turnberry in Ayrshire. When in February 1307 the plumes of smoke were spotted, Bruce began his attempt to win back his crown. He sailed over to Turnberry, part of his Earldom of Carrick, which had been occupied by English troops. Hakon and his fleet had been defeated at Largs by King Alexander III. What fate awaited Bruce and his force of 33 galleys, containing some 300 fighting men?

Now at last I could get back on track with my journey and just like Bruce I would use Arran as my launch point. The tide was out so I headed northwards round Lamlash Bay. I had no idea when the sea was returning so I raced along the shore, not wanting to be caught between any incoming tide and the grass-covered cliffs which met the high water mark. In the shallows, a grey seal bobbed around as I went hopping and jumping (not skipping!) between the rocks and the pools. The whitewashed cottages were shining brightly in the sunshine at Lamlash, the largest village on Arran, where a newly constructed footpath runs all the way into Brodick. Halfway between villages the path summited, allowing a glimpse of the hills of North Arran, the highest of which is Goatfell at 874m. The path continued through the lovely Roots of Arran Community Woodland. Westwards in Gleann Dubh is the site of an ancient fort named as Bruce's castle, which James Douglas made his base following his victory over the garrison of Brodick Castle. Reaching Brodick, I collected my rucksack from the B&B and waited for the ferry.

Sailing away from my mixed fortunes on Arran, I took a seat in the pet friendly section of the ferry. Meg was soon on petting terms with some New Yorkers who were touring Scotland; I chatted to them for a while, asking them questions about their city and their sports teams. They didn't ask me any questions back, so I soon got fed up and shut up. Instead I sat and listened to their small talk, enjoying their accents: listening to them was more fun than talking to them. The weather had been steadily deteriorating all afternoon and it was wretched by the time we bumped up to the pier at Ardrossan. Dilly-dallying around, I was the last foot passenger off the ferry, the crew eventually shooing me ashore. I was in no rush to experience the great outdoors but exiting underneath the raised nose of the heaving bow, I was like a greyhound out of a giant trap; the Ayr Coastal Path awaited and I targeted myself to reach Irvine and rendezvous with a friend.

South Bay was taking a pounding. Waves lashed the promenade; timing was critical to avoid submergence. 'Coastal Path' then became a bit of a misnomer, as the path skirted the shoreline industrial works after Saltcoats, and passed through the towns of Stevenson and Kilwinning. Reaching the River Garnock, I met a couple of guys standing just off the path, supping cans of beer. We got chatting about walking, which they also enjoyed. There were two reasons to go walking, one of them told me. The first was the chance to have a can of beer and the second was to enjoy the scenery. They offered me a drink. I declined and told them about my current plans as well as about my previous walk, following Bonnie Prince Charlie's flight after Culloden. Firstly, they warned me off wild camping near Irvine as it could be a bit unruly at the weekend. Then the 'two reasons' guy said disappointedly: 'I'm 52 and I just found out Jacobites were Tims.'

Taken aback at first, I soon compounded his misery: 'Aye, they were Tories as well!'

I could tell he was drowning in the sea of his busted assumptions, so I tried to pull him up for air: 'But they *were* fighting for Scottish Independence.'

That didn't seem to cut much ice with him either, so I made my goodbyes swift and carried on along the river, eventually reaching Irvine at dinnertime. Near the harbour was the 16th-century Ship Inn, and dogs were welcome in the snug. I met up with my friend Barry, a fellow Robert the Bruce enthusiast. Over a coffee we swapped stories and he gave me some further advice on places in the Galloway Hills connected with Bruce. He also told me about the construction of a medieval village, 'Dun Carron', near my hometown of Falkirk, which for a time he helped build, managing a party of men on community service. He believed that some of the guys had really benefited from the experience and that the work had set them on a positive path. I loved this idea of bringing history to life in a project that must have provided participants with a sense of satisfaction that picking up litter by the roadside never would.

Walking to the shore in the pitch dark, with a strong sea breeze gusting in, I searched amongst the sand dunes to find a sheltered camping spot, confident that the weather would keep any weekend warriors at bay. It certainly did. I had a sleepless night as the wind whipped angrily, testing the tensile strength of my skimpy fabric shelter. Despite six boulders as large as I could scavenge acting as anchors, the tent rolled like a yacht in a hurricane. Even trying to pack up the next morning was a sair fecht, with occasional comic moments as I sprinted over the dunes, chasing bits of clothing or plastic bags torn from my chilled hands. Any remaining weariness from the long night was forgotten as I battled along the beach, against the wind, dwarfed by the high dunes on portside and engulfed by deafening crash of the waves on the starboard side. Some distance ahead lay Troon, where I dreamed of a café by the shore serving a full Scottish breakfast, complete with tea and toast. No such luck, I made do with a beach shelter at South Sands, where I shovelled in some cold snacks. I continued south past the sudden greenery of Royal Troon Golf Club on a stretch of the Smuggler's Path and crossed the Pow Burn at Old Prestwick Golf Club before walking along the top of the dunes to Prestwick and a well-earned early lunch at Café Mancini near the promenade. The owner was being interviewed by a television crew when I went in, so I sat outside with Meg and listened to him regale the presenter with stories of appearing on Chris Evans' TV show, *TFI Friday*. Later, in the town, and by a stroke of pure luck, I came upon Bruce's Well. Robert benefited from the healing waters here and endowed the nearby Spittal and Lazar House ('spittal' meaning hospital and 'lazar', leper). One of the most common legends associated with Bruce is that he suffered from leprosy. He certainly did have bouts of debilitating illness and in later life employed a top Italian physician, Maino de Maineri, to attend to him.[7] An iron fence surrounded the stone steps which descended down to the well so I couldn't partake of the healing waters. Bah!

Skirting round the commercial port, I crossed the River Ayr and headed for Ayr town hall, a fine, classical building supporting a grand octagonal clock spire. Inside, I was led round by a security guard as we searched for Robert the Bruce. Try as we might, we couldn't find him. I thought he was on a stained-glass window but I found out later that what I should have been looking for was a portrait made in bronze by Robert Bryden (1865–1939), a celebrated local artist. As Earl of Carrick, Bruce would have had strong links with Ayr – he destroyed the castle in 1298 during the early years of the Wars of Independence. In 1315, as King of Scots, Bruce held a parliament in the town where the succession was agreed in favour of his brother Edward, rather than to his daughter Marjorie.

I didn't have time to explore – despite the town's ancient heritage, I was rushing through, on my way to Turnberry, to catch up with the King's landing. Reaching the Esplanade, I continued along the coast; ahead lay the remains of Greenan Castle, a 17th-century tower house, and further on, the high cliffs of a headland, the Heads of Ayr. Stopping to read a noticeboard, I discovered that there was no way around this volcanic plug on a high tide. Due to nature's application of Sod's Law, I headed inland along the main road and sought advice at the Heads of Ayr Caravan Park. Directed onto an old railway embankment, I followed this for a while, but I wasn't confident this was an acceptable route; after numerous barbed wire fences and fields of sheep, I got nervous that a farmer might take offence at my travelling with a dog and headed back to the main road again. Cursing my crap research, I took a side road down to Dunure. My mood instantly improved in this scenic village, where a row of 19th-century whitewashed houses with brightly painted lintels overlook a little, square harbour. Just beyond the village are the remains of Dunure Castle, the site of which had been in use since the 13th century, although the current ruins are from a later date. In 1570, the Abbott of Crossraguel Abbey was roasted over an open fire here, after refusing to sign over church lands to the Earl of Cassilis. He survived but never walked again.

Passing below the remnants of the crumbling tower perched on the promontory and clambering over shoreline rocks, I came to yet more impassable cliffs. To escape, I tried climbing up a steep bank where there seemed to be a faint path, but this faded away and I was soon completely surrounded by impenetrable gorse bushes. I retreated downhill and retraced my steps back along the shore before trying again to find a path upwards. It was some fight. I raged within about not having a guidebook, or even any notes, whilst I raged outwardly at the stabbing gorse. Eventually escaping into a livestock field, I found a pillar with a squiggle that represented the Ayr Coastal Path. Following the edge of fields above the cliffs, Meg and I scampered along. In case I was being watched, I kept her on a short leash but knew from experience she was not interested in the sheep. The path deposited me down by the sea again and I spent ages trying to pick a patch of ground on which to pitch my shelter. It was dusk by the time I ate, and Meg began a cruel game that went on intermittently for the duration of the whole walk – staring intently behind me, causing me to turn round in alarm only to find nothing visible. Retreating to my patch of sodden grass, which turned out to have a slope that invited me to cuddle the dog, I fell asleep quickly.

Well rested after an unexpectedly calm night by the shore, I awoke to a cold, bright and beautiful morning. Breaking camp, I was on the

Dunure Castle with Ailsa Craig in the background.

move before 8am – a lack of fresh water meant breakfast was delayed. With the tide out, I made swift progress along the wide beaches watching sea birds hunt and enjoying the warm rays of the rising sun. A few kilometres later, I was at Culzean Bay where I climbed up steps by the gas house (a small stone building where coal gas was produced in the 19th century). Such were my priorities that I gave a wide berth to magnificent Culzean Castle and headed instead for the toilet block to get some much-needed fresh water. The castle is an 18th-century mansion designed by Robert Adam, and was previously owned by the Marquess of Ailsa, Chief of the Kennedy Clan; the chiefs are descendants of Robert the Bruce. In 1945, the castle was handed over to the National Trust for Scotland (to avoid inheritance tax) and is one of the country's top tourist attractions. The castle I was heading for, Turnberry, was the polar opposite to this fine Scottish palace so before I became spoiled, I strode on through the woods of the country park, past Swan Pond, out onto Maidenhead Bay and round to the village of Maidens. From there it was a stroll along the pavement by the main road to Turnberry Golf Course. Crossing the golf course on a public path towards the shore was a serene experience: the golfers quiet in comparison to their attire; the only sounds, the ping of a well hit shot or the occasional phunk of a divvied shot.

From a fragment of Turnberry Castle, looking towards Holy Island and the snow-capped peaks of Arran.

Twelfth-century Turnberry Castle was an impressive clifftop fortification, with sea gates carved from the rock below providing access by boat. Nowadays, a 19th-century Stevenson lighthouse sits amongst much of the ruined foundations. Scrambling over broken walls and buttresses perched on crumbling edges made me giddy, but I found a spot amongst the ruins where I was invisible to all but the sea birds, and prepared a late breakfast. Porridge and water wasn't as fancy as other meals served within these walls, but never was a meal more ravenously consumed. As soon as I had taken off Meg's rucksack to give her a break she rolled on her back to placate an itch, giving me palpitations as she scratched her way towards a vertiginous drop. Across the firth lay the Isle of Arran, a fresh covering of snow on its mountains; standing out clearly in front was Holy Island.

In 1274, Robert the Bruce was born at Turnberry Castle, which had belonged to his mother, a Celtic noble, from whom he inherited the Earldom of Carrick. His father, the 5th Lord of Annandale, was of Norman heritage – the 1st Robert Bruce, who hailed from an area south of Cherbourg, having been granted the fiefdom of Annandale by King David I in 1124. The Bruces also had substantial holdings in

England and were feudal lords of lands between Larne and Glenarm in Ireland.

In 1307, Bruce and his force of 300 men landed nearby; they found confusion because the fire which had inspired him to cross the Clyde was not lit to signal favourable conditions, but belonged to someone else. Bruce was warned that the English were in full control and that the people of Carrick were in no mood for further rebellions. It was Robert's brother, Edward, who steeled the King's heart by saying that now that they were here, they would make a go of it. In such uncertain circumstances began Robert the Bruce's campaign.

The English soldiers based in the area were too many for the castle to hold and some were billeted in the village. There they were attacked and defeated by Bruce's forces. The survivors made for the safety of the castle. Help was sought from Northumberland and a relief force arrived to escort the soldiers and their commander, Henry Percy, back to England.

Bruce slighted Turnberry Castle, a brilliant reversal of the policy he adopted after seizing the crown the previous year when the new King and his supporters had captured castles and tried to hold them. From here onwards, Bruce destroyed castles that he captured as a key aspect of his guerrilla warfare strategy. As well as providing protection to those within, the castle was the centre of civic life: organising local governance, administering law and order, collecting taxes, and otherwise controlling the population would be impossible for an occupying force without a secure fortification to operate from. Thus, Bruce may have been quite satisfied with the current perilous condition of the remains, but I found it sad that the last remnants of the birthplace of one of our national heroes were in such a neglected, unprotected and unloved condition.

The King's landing at Ayrshire was part of a three-pronged strategy. Bruce's younger brothers, Thomas and Alexander, landed at Loch Ryan in Galloway with a second fleet. The third prong was the Bishop of Moray who returned to his diocese, having previously fled to Orkney, to muster support from Bruce's lands in the Garioch, northwest of Aberdeen.

Bruce then headed to the Galloway Hills, a secure base from which

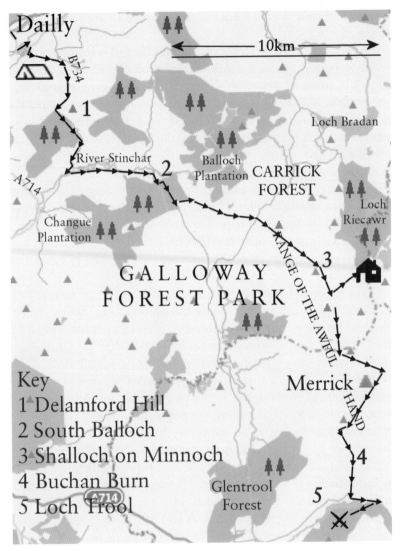

Key
1 Delamford Hill
2 South Balloch
3 Shalloch on Minnoch
4 Buchan Burn
5 Loch Trool

Entering the Galloway Hills.

he could muster support for his cause and link up with his brothers. Trying to keep up, I headed into Turnberry village before following unclassified, quiet back roads in a southeasterly direction. The day remained beautiful and even I couldn't find anything to worry about. I was fed, watered, dry, the walking was easy and I was ahead of schedule. All I needed was some company and a few kilometres later, in the village of Dailly, I met a gruff publican who provided me with the conversation I craved, but either I was a bit naïve with my outpourings or he was just frustrated that the other pub in town was packed out (Meg and I couldn't even get past the smokers at the front lobby). After telling me about the background to this ex-mining community, he poured scorn on my politics and rode roughshod over my thoughts on renewable energy.

The woods at Lindsayton, down by the river, were indeed a quiet spot for camping – my host had been right about that at least. When wild camping, I never like to see anyone else and I don't want to be seen. It was strangely comforting to have the woods all to myself. The plummeting temperature, which eventually bottomed out at -6°C, had probably put people off going for a stroll. I warmed myself with my hobo stove – an old tin can with a few punctures. It allowed me to have a small fire, leaving no trace and could double up as a cooking stove if I ran out of gas. Eventually, the cold chased me to my tent; cocooned in my sleeping bag I was perfectly snug.

In the morning, I followed an underused path crisscrossed with fallen pines out of the woods and onto tarmac once more. The road climbed Delamford Hill where there was an army of droning, whirling turbines. As I walked amongst them, they seemed to march forward with me; reinforcements were always welcome. I descended to the River Stinchar and followed it in an easterly direction, making good time on these quiet highways. The weather was still bright and dry but, ominously, the wind was gaining in intensity. At South Balloch, near the border of Ayrshire and Galloway, the road turned southwards to contour along the wooded slopes of Bencallen before I went off-piste, using the gap in the forestry plantation created for the electricity pylons to continue east. The going was incredibly rough, the undergrowth varying from knee to waist high. Meg bounded along, continuously disappearing then re-emerging. On Pinbreck Hill, at the edge of the plantation, amongst the harvested remains of a section of forest, I felt the full force of the punching wind. Escaping gradually, I headed downhill to little Aldinna Loch, stumps and logs giving way to heather and peat bogs. Already this difficult ground was putting a strain on me and by the time I climbed upwards on the tussocky grass surrounding Eldrick Hill I was blowing hard. When I reached the foot slopes of Shalloch on Minnoch, the proper beginning of my sortie into the Galloway Hills, my body felt like it already completed a triathlon.

Resembling the Highlands, but with even fewer inhabitants, the Galloway Hills are remote, rough, difficult, wild and full of adventurous possibilities. Bruce's hideaway was in Glen Trool away to the south and I wanted to approach it via a group of hills known as 'The Range of the Awful Hand'. I climbed steadily on uneven grassy tussocks, the standard underfoot condition on lower slopes, and the headwind grew stronger as I reached onto Shalloch, an outlying top of a long, north–south ridge. Next, I headed towards similarly named Shalloch on Minnoch and although the ascent was steady on the dome-shaped hill, the wind was making the going very difficult and sapping my remaining energy. I screamed out encouragements to myself that were swallowed whole by the assaulting gale. With only 120 metres of climbing to go I reached the snowline where there was a thin coverage, the top layer of which was lying in icy balls. Every few minutes a particularly strong gust of wind would blow the top surface off in clouds, straight towards me. Each time I was overwhelmed and hunkered down to wait on it passing, thousands of particles stung my exposed face. Meg, who always walked ahead, would turn away from the wind and stare at me, her eyes narrowed accusingly. As the climb eased, the thundering wind increased its ferocity and on the summit plateau, I couldn't stand upright; almost bent double and unable even to properly draw breath, I stumbled onwards, because only a short distance ahead was the trig point and a shelter built from cairn rocks. Reaching the circular den, I collapsed inside, gasping for air and chilled to the bone – suddenly, the violence of the turbulent air that had almost overwhelmed me was

Climbing up to Shalloch on Minnoch in the Galloway Hills.

removed and I turned over and lay back on my rucksack, dizzy from the release. Wow, what a start, I thought; and that was only the first finger, the bloody pinkie of the Awful Hand.

In the bitter cold it could only be a short rest. I headed south, Tarfessock the next target and the wind lessened quickly as I descended off the summit. Reaching a bealach, Nick of the Carclach, I looked around and a tiny cottage off to my left, 320m below and only a couple of kilometres away, caught my eye. I glanced at the map: Tunskeen Bothy. It was late afternoon and I had already decided that Tarfessock would be my last hill of the day before heading down to a forest for shelter. Opting for a bothy and the chance to get a roof over my head was a no-brainer. Prior to my journey I had heard that some of the Galloway bothies were in poor condition, having been abused by people using them as party places. Back in Irvine, my friend Barry had told me that as far as he knew the bothies were all open and in OK condition. Also it was a Monday and who parties on a Monday? I headed downhill through the Nick, the eastern face of the ridge, completely different to the rounded western slopes. This side was all

Tunskeen Bothy, an unexpected haven.

cliffs, steep slopes and rocky outcrops, which made for a quick, if dar-ing, descent. Even on the lower slopes the going remained tricky, the broken, uneven ground making each step a challenge. I didn't berate myself for coming so far off the ridge and losing all this height; deep down, I knew it was the right choice. I followed as close as I could to a burn, the banks of which were rockier, meaning less awkward vegetation to negotiate. Stepping between rocks and jumping with my sticks to support me, I was able to overtake Meg. Low enough to be out of the wind, I was charging on, hell-bent on reaching the bothy, when the sound of frantic scraping turned my head. Meg had almost disappeared down a hole between the rocks. Her front legs, head and shoulders were all that remained visible and her legs were going like the clappers as she tried to stay up. I dived back and grabbed her col-lar, preventing her from falling further in. Then an adrenalin boosted heave and she popped out with her rucksack hanging off her back legs. None the worse for her mishap, I returned to the dark hole and realised she had had a lucky escape: when I poked downwards with one of my walking sticks it disappeared into a void!

Happily, there was no smoke as I approached the whitewashed

cottage. The door was unlocked and the place was empty. No numpties on quad bikes after all! The bothy was a tidy single room, spartanly furnished and with a powerful stove. In the corner lay sticks, logs and a bag of coal. At each side of the room were the usual wooden benches for sleeping and a few chairs for sitting round the fireside. Perfect! Hanging up my waterproofs to dry, I got down to domestic duties. The stove was choked and it looked like the last fire prepared on it had failed to take. After clearing out two full buckets of ash, I separated the sticks and logs into size order and set the fire. I was carrying Vaseline balls (Not a solution to a friction problem, just cotton wool soaked in the petroleum jelly) and they helped get a blaze going quickly. Soon I was sitting in front of a roaring heat, deliriously happy, whilst the wind and rain raged outside.

Bruce's situation was otherwise when he arrived in the Galloway Hills. He learned that his siblings met with disaster as they landed at Galloway, and were defeated by a force of Galwegians, loyal to the Comyns and headed by Dungal MacDouall. Thomas and Alexander were taken to Carlisle, where they were hung and beheaded. This defeat added to the vulnerability of the King's position and he soon found himself trapped within the hills, completely surrounded by foes, both Scottish and English. The King was also made aware of the disaster that had befallen another of his brothers, Neil, and his charges, the womenfolk of Bruce's party who were separated from the King after the Battle of Dalrigh. Neil was captured while holding Kildrummy Castle in Aberdeenshire and sent to England, where he was drawn, hung and beheaded. The womenfolk who had escaped prior to the siege fled north, accompanied by the Earl of Atholl. They were captured by the Earl of Ross whilst claiming sanctuary at Saint Duthac's chapel in Tain, and escorted to England. The Earl of Atholl was hung (the first earl to be executed in England for 230 years) and the fate of some of the women is infamous. Bruce's sister Mary and the Countess Isabel of Buchan (who had placed the crown on Bruce's head at his coronation) were lodged in cages hung from the battlements of Roxburgh and Berwick castles respectively, so that passers-by could stare at them. Bruce's wife, Elizabeth, and his daughter, Marjorie, were also held prisoner, although in less extreme circumstances. The King would also have learned that many of his supporters captured at the Battle of Methven or thereafter had been executed. These were truly dark days for Robert the Bruce. His family, friends and supporters were paying a terrible price for his seizing of the throne. It behoved of him to do everything in his power to prove that they had not invested their all, for nothing. However, he had but a few lads in the Galloway Hills, while his enemy had the combined power of England, Scotland, Wales and Ireland.

If ever there was a spider moment for Bruce, this was it. The apocryphal story is that Bruce was hiding in a cave after yet another defeat. As he contemplated the disasters that had befallen him, he noticed a spider attempting to build a web and was encouraged by its refusal to accept defeat in its attempts. The number of failed attempts of the spider matched the number of defeats suffered by Bruce. The spider eventually managed to cling to a stone wall of the cave on its seventh attempt. The King, encouraged, resolved to carry on the struggle.

One glimmer of hope for the Scottish King was the very ferocity of Edward's treatment of his supporters which, as Barrow explains, may actually have contributed towards continued support for King Robert because there was no option for Bruce supporters to switch sides.

Next morning, I slowly retraced my steps along the difficult ground and with a steep final pull got myself back onto the ridge. The wind was nowhere near as strong as previously and the first rise of the day, Tarfessock (the ring finger of the Awful Hand), came and went easily. Kirriereoch, the next top (middle finger) was a tougher proposition; I climbed up its steep face among snow-capped and icy rocks, not out of my depth but at my limit given the conditions and the pack I was carrying. The top was mist-covered, so I took a compass bearing on the bald, flat hilltop to locate the summit cairn. As I descended, the sky cleared briefly, showing me the shape of Merrick and its outlier, the Little Spear. Having seen the route of my next ascent, however briefly, I confidently strode onwards and upwards into the mist again. I tottered along a short, knife-edge ridge which connected the hump of

Little Spear with the main summit of Merrick (forefinger) and rested in another shelter, hoping once more for a short break in the weather; but the mist didn't clear for me a second time. Merrick is the highest peak in the Southern Uplands at 843m, but there were no views of England, Ireland or The Isle of Man for me.

I continued southwards over Benyellary, the thumb of the Awful Hand, and followed a good path (Merrick is usually climbed from this side) down by the Whiteland Burn. I had my lunch at another bothy, Culsharg. Fine as it was to be out of the elements for a time, the bothy was barren and lifeless. Without company or a fire, perched on a log, staring at the bare walls whilst cooking over a crude bench was only practical, not enjoyable. There was a book lying beside the blackened fireplace. Exactly what I needed! I turned it over with trepidation and damn, it was a Jeremy Clarkson! However, it wasn't as bad as it could have been: the first 33 pages were ripped out. The bothy got the better end of the bargain. I left behind William McIlvanney's tough cop, Laidlaw, and *The Papers of Tony Veitch*.

I caught up with Robert Bruce shortly afterwards at the Buchan Burn, where he was accosted by a large party of Galloway men. Bruce had only one attendant with him, whom he sent away to get help. Holding off his enemies single-handedly, guarding a narrow ford of the burn, the King was able to fight on a one-to-one basis with man after man until a pile of bodies lay before him. After his companion returned with reinforcements, the Galloway men backed off. This is one of a number of heroic encounters written about in Barbour's poem. Obviously greatly exaggerated (Barbour tells us Bruce held off 200 men) to enhance Bruce's martial prowess, perhaps to balance the bad publicity of earlier behaviour – Bruce had swapped sides during the Wars of Independence and of course murdered John Comyn in a church. No doubt many of the adventures were based in fact, but despite the exaggeration it seems miraculous that Bruce survived an incredibly perilous time in the Galloway Hills.

Just a few moments later I was standing overlooking beautiful Loch Trool in the same position as Bruce had stood in 1307 before the skirmish at Glen Trool. It was the King's first victory in the field

The Buchan Burn, where Bruce held up a party of enemies.

following his return from exile and an early example of his tactical genius and ability to use the terrain to his advantage. Aymer de Valence, the Earl of Pembroke, the victor at the Battle of Methven, was searching for Bruce with a large party of horsemen. On the southern shores of Loch Trool awaited the King's force. At the sound of the Bruce's horn, the Scots, hidden higher up the steep slopes of the glen, rolled boulders down onto the cavalry moving in a narrow formation by the loch side. Next the Scots sent a volley of arrows down upon distraught men and injured mounts. Charging down on a wide front, Bruce's men caused maximum damage on the English who were unable to bring their horses to bear on the attackers, stuck as they were on a narrow track. De Valence's forces were routed and pursued. For Bruce a large-scale victory at last, after all the defeats and losses. In terms of morale and recruiting power, it became a great victory.

Bruce is thought to have managed the ambush from a high vantage point on the north side of the loch, where there is now a large, inscribed stone commemorating the conflict. From the stone and accompanying

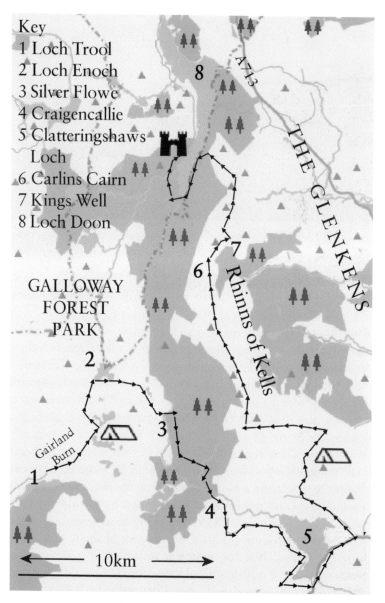

Key
1 Loch Trool
2 Loch Enoch
3 Silver Flowe
4 Craigencallie
5 Clatteringshaws
  Loch
6 Carlins Cairn
7 Kings Well
8 Loch Doon

THE GLENKENS

GALLOWAY
FOREST
PARK

Rhinns of Kells

Gairland Burn

10km

Adventures in the Galloway Hills.

The skirmish at Loch Trool took place on the far side of the loch: while English forces followed a lochside path, Bruce's men were hidden on the steep, now forested, slopes,

information boards, I walked downhill through oak woodland, round the head of the loch to the site of the ambush. As I stood near the water, I looked up the slopes as the English must have done when they heard the shouts of the Scots and the rumbling, crashing sounds of tumbling rocks. It would have been mayhem as the attackers followed the boulders downhill and launched themselves into the flanks of the panicking horses. Even imagining such violent activity in this beautiful natural setting seemed an abomination; the only movement on the steep slopes now was that of two feral goats feeding peacefully on secure ground. At the head of the loch is a grassy area known as the Soldiers' Holm, where reputedly the bodies of the slain were buried.

In the golden glow of late afternoon sunlight, lathered in sweat, I headed north, picking up a footpath that took me into a hanging valley down which the Gairland Burn falls. I camped by the marshy shores of peaceful Loch Valley, which despite being at a height of 330m is sheltered by the surrounding hills. On a tiny bit of sandy beach, I ate, watching the sunset reflect on the calm waters. It was beautiful end to a productive day. I was now firmly ensconced within the bosom of these hills, loving the remote feeling and the sense that I had the wildness to myself. As darkness unfolded, loneliness set in and I scurried back to my tent, where I had Mr Clarkson for company.

I rose early and this time I had breakfast with the moon for company. It was turning into a beautiful day as I continued on towards Loch Neldricken (Loch of the Ambush). Climbing up to this loch using a narrow channel and finding a whole landscape opening up in front of me it truly felt, on this clear bright morning, like the land that time forgot. In front of me lay the shallow loch, where rocks and grasses broke the otherwise still surface; surrounding it were steep-sided hills, the peak of Craignairny dominating the distant skyline. If a Pterodactyl had flown over my head I wouldn't have batted an eyelid. Stepping lightly, I passed by on the west side round an inlet called the 'Murder Hole'; novelist SR Crocket used this location in *The Raiders* as a place where the bodies of robbery victims were dumped. Following a cleft in the hillside along which ran a faint path, I moseyed uphill towards Loch Enoch. A series of Bruce's heroic, semi-legendary, adventures has been placed in this area. Given the names of the natural features, it is hardly surprising. The tales are told by Barbour and promote Bruce's individual skills and courage.[8] The incident I was partially through recreating was where Bruce was pursued from Glen Trool to Loch Enoch by a force of Galwegians under John MacDougall, his conqueror at Dalrigh. The King must have been fit and hardy to have kept ahead of those nimble Galwegians, who would have been much more used to this terrain.

I arrived at the heart of wildness, Loch Enoch, which is completely encapsulated by surrounding hills. Snow-dusted Merrick hardly looked 843m high but then the loch itself was at an altitude of 500m. The crazily shaped loch contained small, heather-clad islands, one of which contained *its* own lochan. The gorgeous white sands round the dark water's edge were famous for sharpening tools. Bruce and his followers would have known to have sharpened their weapons here. This was a blissful, calm and serene place and I ambled along, watched by a couple of inquisitive Canada geese, with the water lapping onto my shoes, my lonely footprints following the ins and outs of the beach. On the particular occasion that I was following in Bruce's footsteps, he arrived in the vicinity to find that a second body of men were approach-

Sandy shoreline at Loch Enoch.
Arriving here, Bruce found himself trapped between two forces.

ing from the north. Bruce split up his own small group and with just his brother-in-law for company he headed east to a pass in the hills.

At the loch's southeast corner I climbed a short distance to a ridge connecting the hills of Craignairny and Craig Neldricken, contoured round to the south of Craignairny and clambered down some big slabs of granite. From the bealach known as the 'Nick of the Dungeon' I then descended towards a large area of blanket bog known as the Silver Flowe, a national nature reserve.

The group of chasing Galwegians had a bloodhound that once belonged to Bruce and when he split his party, the hound faithfully followed its master. John MacDougall sent five of his quickest men ahead to try and catch up with the King. These five were despatched by the fugitives, but the hound they could not shake. Crossing the Silver Flowe, Bruce and his relative ran down the Cooran Lane burn to try and put the hound off the scent before finally the King shot the hound with an arrow and escaped.

At the valley floor beside Loch Dungeon and under the giant cliffs of Craignaw, I began crossing the blanket bog, the ground occasion-ally quivering unnervingly below me. In the distance a herd of red deer were feeding and drinking on habitat unchanged for thousands of years. Bruce and his brother-in-law would have struggled just as much as I did through deep grasses, awkward tussocks and marshy pools. The going eased slightly alongside the Brishie Burn, which I followed for a time, but eventually the frustration of slow going on awkward ground beat me. I still had a long way to go and I headed towards the Saugh Burn, which I crossed at a ford before making for a forest road on the far side of the Cooran Lane. At the edge of the reserve, a sign belatedly warned me that the Silver Flowe was hazardous due to its wet and fragile nature. Back on solid ground, I squeezed the water from my socks and shoes and began a forced march, following the line of the Cooran Lane, but from a distance.

Another story relates that Bruce and his companion met three vagabonds as they fled this area. These three men joined up with them and at the end of the day shared their meat with the exhausted pair. Suspicious of their motives, Bruce, told his brother-in-law to remain on guard while he slept. Unfortunately, he too fell asleep and the King was startled awake in the nick of time to fend off and ultimately kill the three assailants. His brother-in-law didn't survive the melee.

Many kilometres of forest road later and just as the King had done, I arrived on my own at the farm of Craigencaille. Here Bruce met a widow who had three sons, each to different fathers. (What happened to the three fathers is unrecorded, but open to speculation!) When she found out the identity of the wanderer at her door, the woman offered Bruce the service of the three young men, McKie, Murdoch and McLurg, who each proved their archery ability to the King by shooting ravens in the cliffs above the farm. Bruce's Wa's, recorded in the area of the farm, were reputed to be walls built from the stones of the house in which the King was given shelter.[9]

The rest of the afternoon was spent reaching Clatteringshaws Loch, mainly travelling along an unclassified public road. Arriving at the brand new visitor centre car park with a few minutes to spare before closing, I got talking to a biker from Prestwick; my first proper

Clatteringshaws Loch. The water levels were raised in 1935 with the building of a dam.

conversation for three days. As I was moaning about the difficult going underfoot, he told me the grassy tussocks were known as 'Dougals'. I could see the resemblance with the dog from *The Magic Roundabout* and thereafter the tussocks were never quite such a nuisance again, now that they had been associated with a happy childhood memory. Rejuvenated by a freshly brewed coffee and scone in the visitor centre café, I followed a footpath to Bruce's Stone.

Bruce rested against this granite stone after the battle. The information board says that he swept upon an English army at dawn while they slept. Another addition to this story is that during the battle and with the sun behind them, the sons of the widow of Craigencaille drove a herd of goats over the hills. The English thought that it was Scottish reinforcements, lost heart and fled the battlefield. Before Clatteringshaws Loch was created with the building of a dam, local tales told of farmers digging up weapons in the fields.

The legendary tales I have related confirm Bruce's martial ability and certainly he proved himself a master of guerrilla warfare. During his brief exile, he must have thought long and hard about his defeats and William Wallace's victories, before realising that when the Scots had won against numerically superior and better-armed opponents it was down to tactical advantage gained by taking the initiative. Did Bruce suddenly learn all the lessons of the previous ten years, did he have an able group of lieutenants who between them came up with battle plans, or did someone teach him? As Dr Fiona Watson says of Bruce: 'in 1306 he went away so rubbish and came back in 1307 so great'.

I continued round the loch, heading north, and joined up with the Southern Upland Way for a few kilometres. When I was too exhausted to walk any further, I camped in the only flat piece of ground in sight, right on top of the path.

The next morning I was up early again, before someone walked over the top of me. I was looking forward to meeting up with my compadre, George, at a Bruce stronghold: Loch Doon Castle. Between us, here on the eastern fringes of the Galloway Forest Park, was the Rhinns of Kells; a ridge of hills with eight tops at a height of 600–800m. From the farm at Clenrie, I started to climb; underfoot, the inevitable Dougals and heather eventually gave way to short grasses and exposed rock. As I gained the ridge at an outlying top, Meikle Lump, the conditions were becoming subarctic: perishing cold, frozen ground underfoot and high winds. By the time I made the first proper top, Meikle Millyea, I was fully exposed to the wind and it was ferocious! I felt like a polar explorer as I fought for every step along the ridge: leaning into the wind, using my poles for balance; carrying a large rucksack with the straps flapping crazily; wearing all my clothing including a black balaclava, with only my eyes exposed to the elements. Meg too struggled. Whenever the wind blew the rucksack off her back, it entangled itself under her midriff. Descending between tops, there was respite and a chance to strengthen the resolve before the next battle. There was no realistic low level alternative to my route so I didn't waver from the task. Every top was a mini-victory.

The fifth top was Carlin's Cairn. The buffeting wind was causing me to veer unintentionally and disconcertingly over towards the steep

From the summit of Coserine (814m), looking towards Carlin's Cairn.

western slopes. The giant summit cairn ahead was another raison d'etre. It was built in tribute to Bruce by a grateful family to whom the King granted land in thanks for their help during his darkest hours. There was a shelter scooped out from the cairn and *was I grateful* for that! As on Shalloch on Minnoch a couple of days previously, the sudden calmness was quite dizzying. The next top was Meal, on the northeastern flank of which was a spring called King's Well and a stone called King's Seat. Descending from the summit of Meal, on a compass bearing whilst counting steps, my mind wandered. When I came out of my dwam, I had forgotten how far I had come. Nevertheless, I had a good look around what I thought was the approximate location of the stone, but the hillside was covered in imposters and I could see no water. Bruce reputedly sat on the stone whilst drinking from the spring. I will have to leave that to others to send me their photographs.

Descending from the final top, Coran of Portmark, I walked down a gentle spur to Loch Doon, rejoicing in the still air. Hair wrenching frustration soon replaced my contentment. Just when I expected an easy end to a hard day, I found the lochside path round to the southern tip of Loch Doon to be nonexistent; more Dougals, forestry plantations, long grass and boggy ground – tears of despair from yet more slow going welled up in my eyes.

Finally rounding Loch Doon, I picked up a forest road, but delight turned to dismay as the rain started and for the last three kilometres of my day, it absolutely hammered down. As I neared the fort, a lady from a roadside cottage came out and told me that she was storing a bag of my provisions. George had dropped off a bag with her and would be with me shortly. Taking shelter in her porch, I eked out a conversation with her husband, glad of the temporary respite from the weather. When I could delay no longer without being rude, the couple had, after all, done me a favour, I walked along to the roofless castle to wait for my friend.

Loch Doon Castle, built in the 13th century, was one of the key fortifications of Bruce's Earldom of Carrick. When he was crowned in 1306, he provisioned this castle intending it to be a key stronghold. After the collapse of his kingship, the castle was captured by the opposition. Robert's brother-in-law, Sir Christopher Seton, was found inside, sent to Newcastle and executed. During 1307, as Bruce hid out in the surrounding hills, this castle was held against him and was not recovered until some years later.

Originally situated in the middle of the loch, the exterior of the

Loch Doon Castle, which was rebuilt on the shore of the loch.

castle was dismantled in the 1930s when a hydroelectric scheme was planned which would raise the water level. Many of the interior walls were left behind and can still be seen on the little island nearby. Although quite small, it was well and expensively constructed with fine ashlar masonry (regular shaped blocks of cut stone). In an approximate polygonal shape, the 11 sides formed a strong curtain wall.

Outside the castle, I put my walking poles in a cross shape by the road and waited for my mate within. Eventually he came toddling along and a sense of joy engulfed me at the sight of my old friend. In George's company I could let rip about the ups and downs so far but considering how poorly I felt at the outset, I didn't complain too much. It was just so reassuring to be able to relax with a friend. As we chatted about normal stuff, I knew within myself that I was getting into the walk now and that the mental strength was building up. I took confidence from the fact that I had met the challenges of the Galloway Hills.

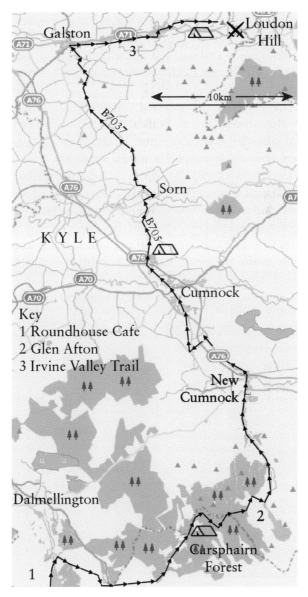

Loch Doon to Loudon Hill.

CHAPTER 3

Heading North

THE FOLLOWING MORNING, we walked along Loch Doon and George incentivised me with the promise of a café at the foot of the loch. This seemed unlikely given the remote location, but I took him at his word and envisaged a fresh cup of coffee and a porcelain toilet. Loch Doon is the largest freshwater loch in southern Scotland and is shaped like a gigantic leaping salmon. Although remote by today's standards, set amongst hills and forest, the area has been settled by man for 6,000 years. In the Middle Ages, the area warranted the building of an expensive castle in the centre of the loch. The portcullis is said to lie beneath the dark murky waters. In 1823, six ancient canoes were discovered, submerged in the loch; within the canoes were a war club and a Viking battleaxe. More recently, in 1982, after a six-year search, a Spitfire was recovered from the loch. It had crashed in 1941, killing the Czech pilot on his first solo flight. The wreckage, including a well preserved engine, is now in the care of Dumfries and Galloway Aviation Museum.

The variety of birds caught my naturalist friend's eye and where I would have identified a couple of species, George easily pointed out oystercatchers, greylag geese, a heron, pied wagtails, meadow pipits, starlings and chaffinches.

Sure enough, there was a cosy little café: The Roundhouse. We met Fran, a twitcher from Ayrshire who was keeping an eye on an osprey nest on the other side of the loch – hoping to see a pair return after a winter in Africa. Along with Brian, the café owner, we had a chat over Americanos and lattès; despite talking incessantly to George, my tongue still had a lot of catching up to do. Brian told me some of the history of the area. On one occasion, when Loch Doon Castle was under attack, the besiegers created a dam to raise the water level. One of the defenders was offered a reward to swim out from the castle and break the dam; this he did, but was promptly swept away by the force of the water. However, his family were still given the piece of ground that had been offered as a reward to the brave swimmer, known thereafter as the Promised Land. Before leaving, George had a look for the ospreys through Fran's £1,700 Swarovski binoculars; I didn't trust my butterfingers. A few days later, Fran's investment and his efforts were rewarded when he spotted an osprey returning to its nest. Soon Mum and Dad were both on the scene, and in the summer two chicks were born.

Heading east, we crossed a small area of moorland and our approach to Loch Muck was greeted with the haunting, beautiful call of the curlews, which I absolutely adore. A kestrel and a great spotted woodpecker were added to our list before the weather took a turn for the worse and driving rain became the predominant condition of the afternoon's climate. At least I had company. Snatched pieces of conversation passed the time as we followed the Water of Deugh into Carsphairn Forest. Walking through the large plantation there wasn't a lot to divert our attention, not that we were looking. Despite some shelter from the trees, we had our heads pointed down to our toes. We called it a day when, still within the woods, we reached the Fingland Burn and found a level piece of cleared ground, only a couple of kilometres short of our intended target, Glen Afton, which was another of Bruce's hiding places. During a brief dry spell, we took the opportunity to get the tents up and eat before the rain returned and forced an early retiral.

In the morning, George returned to his car. His company, during rotten conditions, had kept my spirits up. I soldiered on and soon turned off the forest road and onto what, according to the map, should have been a footpath. However, it had been obliterated by bulldozer tracks, so I hopped along until I regained the track at a break in the trees, where a marshy, Dougal-infested channel guided me along to Glen Lee cottage. Reaching the roofless ruin, I found a small river blocking my way. This was a surprise! I looked at my map more closely and saw that a thick, black boundary-line hid the blue line of the Water of Deugh. Cursing, I removed my socks and

Glen Afton and left of centre the rock face known as Stayamera.

shoes and hitched up the breeks. Using a hiking pole for balance, I waded through the freezing water and deposited my pack before crossing back to pick up the dog. I stumbled over for a third time with numb feet and a wriggling companion. Conifers were overgrown around the ruin, but breaking through the trees I found a clearing, which the all but invisible path had probably followed at one time. At the Sandy Syke Burn I lost the route of the path once more, so I followed the water until I came to a fire break, which I used to exit the forest. I found myself high up on the west side of Glen Afton, a long, remote and steep-sided glen through which flowed the Afton Water, made famous by Robert Burns' song 'Sweet Afton'. Almost 500 years before Burns visited, Robert the Bruce was taking shelter at the head of the glen. I began to descend. As I crossed some fields, a farmer on a quad bike, tailed by a small collie dog, made a beeline for me. Initially he was suspicious of my intentions, taking me for a poacher, but Meg helped to break the ice. After I explained my purpose, the farmer pointed out Castle William, a rocky outcrop at the head of the glen, associated with William Wallace. I asked him about Stayamer Brae, a large rock face on Craigbraneoch Hill on the other side of the glen. He thought the name was strange and out of keeping with local area. Possibly the name derives from 'Stay Aymer', ie Aymer de Valence, Earl of Pembroke, Edward's governor, who was charged with capturing Bruce. At this brae, maybe he was unable to apprehend or even approach a well defended Robert the Bruce.

In August 1307, James Douglas came to Glen Afton to warn Bruce that King Edward II of England was at nearby Cumnock Castle. Edward's father, Edward I, had died leading a great army into Scotland to destroy King Hobbe (fool), once and for all. Edward junior rather unwillingly took up the reins and marched the army as far as Cumnock Castle but no further. He stayed for a number of days, failed to find Bruce, achieved nothing else of purpose and returned to England and his coronation.

The death of Edward I was a massive boost to Bruce, who was now at last starting to ascend from the trough in which he had been stuck. As well as conquering Scotland, Edward had added Wales to his kingdom. With England having a strong presence in Ireland, Edward very nearly united the whole of the British Isles, 400 years earlier than it eventually happened. He dominated Scotland from 1296 to 1307 but his son, Edward II, turned out to be a very a poor successor. A bit of timely yin and yang for Scotland!

Leaving the glen I came to New Cumnock, an ex-mining town. With some tumbleweed, the place could have been an American midwest town after the gold rush had passed through. New Cumnock's gold had been coal and now it looked like the business owners were selling up and moving on. Lots of the property sales were going to auction, surely not a good sign. I stopped to buy a newspaper and lingered happily, parked immobile on a bench with a few snacks, the back pages and a spot of sunshine. Cumnock Castle, Edward II's temporary base, overlooked the confluence of the River Nith and the Afton Water, just to the west of the main street. There is nothing left of the castle and now the Auld Kirk occupies the site.

I intended to use back roads to reach Cumnock, en route to Galston, another of Bruce's bases in 1307, but the A76 has a pavement alongside it for two-thirds of the way, so I made use of that before retiring to the back roads. In Cumnock, I caught up with some urgent emails by the Old Church in the square, where kids were playing on the steps of the mercat cross, the square shaft of which dates back to 1509. By the end of the day, I had reached Auchinleck and camped in a community woodland on the outskirts of the village.

Crossing the River Ayr, one of the main barriers north, at the pretty little village of Sorn, I came to the Olive Tree Café. Meg and I received a warm welcome, so instead of just a ordering a coffee to go, I sat in and had a full breakfast, only a couple of hours since having consumed half a litre of porridge and a packet of cereal biscuits. Despite eating 4,000 calories per day I was always ready for more food. Thankfully, my man boobs, which had been a bit noticeable in some of the photographs that appeared in the newspapers before I left, were disappearing fast. As I awaited my food, Meg got some titbits and the café owner, Martin, entertained us with stories of a newborn lamb which he had adopted. It wasn't being reared for his menu, it was to be a pet-company for a pig, two dalmatians, a basset hound and a duck. After this civilised breakfast, my hunger was at last totally satisfied. This in turn engendered a drowsy desire to linger in the sun-drenched conservatory.

The thought of the miles that lay ahead got me under way once more and I marched along quiet back roads Galston; Sir William Keith, a prominent knight during the Wars of Independence, hailed from this place. In 1330, he brought Bruce's heart back from Spain after the death at the Battle of Teba of Sir James Douglas, its protector – an act which is commemorated on the town's coat of arms.

Back in 1307, Robert the Bruce's strength must have been growing as he took himself out of the remote hills of Galloway to base himself here at Galston. With increasing numbers flocking to his banner, he took on an English force in a set battle at nearby Loudon Hill, my next objective. Leaving tarmac behind, I sauntered along the River Irvine, following the Irvine Valley Trail. It was quiet and pleasant walking, but my peace was shattered at Newmilns when I went to buy some water at a local convenience store. Two guys were at the checkout and I was nearby at the drinks fridge. The young girl at the checkout charged them for the two cans of beer they had tried to hide. When they found out they were being charged for the cans, the men were livid and one of them shouted towards the back of the shop: 'Hey Tony, better get your staff sorted out ya black bastard or yer windaes are getting panned in.'

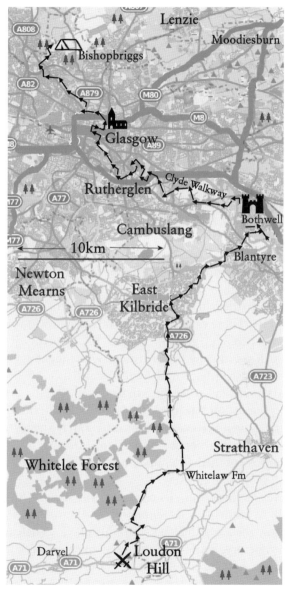

Loudon Hill to Glasgow.

The brave girl behind the checkout didn't flinch – even though there must have been at least three crimes in this one sentence. The guys paid up and left before Tony could catch them; spooked, I also paid up, and rushed outside to check that Meg hadn't been given a kick as they left.

Normal service was resumed as I walked along an avenue of mature trees by Lanfine estate. In due course I crossed the River Irvine on the Randolcoup Bridge and continued through the village of Darvel. On top of an old railway embankment, with the massive prominence of Loudon Hill close by, I called it a day.

In May 1307, Bruce fought a more typical pitched battle against English forces at the Battle of Loudon Hill. Although his troops were vastly outnumbered, they were in a strong defensive position, partially protected by the giant volcanic plug, as they awaited the English army approaching along the Bothwell to Ayr road.

Bruce's dug-in troops were positioned so that the natural terrain prevented the English cavalry from charging on a wide front against them and the battlefield was enhanced to the Scot's advantage by the digging of pits. These caused the English vanguard to narrow further as it approached and greatly reduced the impetus of the cavalry charge, which was met by Bruce's troops who fought aggressively. The English were pushed back and Aymer de Valence, their commander, was forced to turn tail and return to Bothwell.

Duncan's notes on Barbour's *Bruce* offer an alternative viewpoint on the battle as well as some extra information. He believes the English were travelling in the opposite direction, from Ayr to Bothwell and that the purpose of the battle was for Bruce to appropriate the money bags which they were carrying.[10]

Whatever the direction, the result was the same: a Scottish victory on the field of battle. Bruce's reputation and stature was growing and he was surely shedding the baggage of his previous defeats. However, despite this victory, Bruce was still very much an outlaw in his own country. Gains he made could not be consolidated, surrounded as he was by so many enemies, both domestic and foreign. In September 1307, Aymer de Valence was replaced as Governor of Scotland by John

Loudon Hill shrouded in mist.

of Brittany and Bruce used the temporary power vacuum to break out of the southwest. The northeast of Scotland had been suitably stirred up by the Bishop of Moray, and Bruce's victories would have enhanced his reputation in a part of the country ruled by English Sheriffs but not yet tired of the ravages of war that the southwest had endured. Bruce gathered his followers and headed north to make use of this support and begin a campaign to reduce the power of his domestic enemies. Only with a united Scotland would Bruce have any chance of long-term success against the forces of Edward II.

I climbed the steep inclines of Loudon Hill to survey the scene of the battle on the sloping ground to the south, but my view was obscured by a strange haze; for the third day on the trot it was bright and dry, but strangely overcast, with the sun hidden from view. I wasn't sure if it was a local weather condition or not; it reminded me of industrial smog. It was my time now to break out of Ayrshire, cross the Central Belt, and head for Argyll.

Following country roads, the walking became tedious as the terrain was fairly featureless. I had an early lunch in a mucky field where my low motivation caused me to be careless and I managed to melt a hole in my plastic eating bowl. Later, when the caffeine kicked in and I saw East Kilbride ahead, I felt an upsurge in my mood – walking through a large town would be a variation to my usual routine, and I needed some distraction. Humiliatingly, it turned out I was to be the distraction, as folk slowed down to laugh and point at me and the dog. I already knew that Meg's rucksack often caused hilarity, and unless I had some embarrassing appendage to my own rucksack, then Meg was probably the cause of much mirth, but it made me feel really self-conscious. At 3pm, Meg and I walked past a primary school where parents huddled outside the gates, waiting. I could feel the stares. Mums and dads were thinking – big rucksack, armed with sticks, grubby looking, and a dog with potential suicide vest. I felt guilty invading their world and I also felt like a total plonker; one wrong move and I knew I would be at the bottom of a parent pile-on. Next, I passed a secondary school just as the hordes emerged and I felt equally out of place, bobbing along head and shoulders above the shoving masses. Desperate now to escape this urban hell, I walked through a housing scheme and descended down to Calder Glen, where a footpath ran alongside the River Calder. Here at least I felt comfortable, but all too soon I reached a dead end where the river flowed under the Hamilton Expressway. Climbing up to the road, I was desperate to escape and this maybe was my final challenge, a stupid and almost suicidal crossing of the Hamilton expressway at a time of peak traffic.

At Blantyre, the birthplace of David Livingstone, I crossed the River Clyde on a pedestrian bridge named after the great Victorian explorer. Walking into Bothwell at around 5pm, my urban misery continued. I had decided to try and get a B&B, as it didn't look like wild camping would be possible near the town. Looking for accommodation on the High Street, I received, for no earthly reason, a one finger salute and a snarl from a passing motorist. Another guy leaned out of his accomplice's car and shouted: 'Have you got a body in that pack, pal?' My sense of humour had long since vanished, only to be replaced with an overblown self-consciousness, and all I could do was stare grimly at the laughing youths. Finding no B&Bs and feeling uncomfortable as hell, I turned around and walked back down the other side of the street, where there were plenty of nice boutique-style shops all closing up for the night; pretty owners looked concerned as I walked by and hurriedly turned the locks. Finally my eye caught a glimpse

Climbing up towards Bothwell Castle.

of a Douglas Shield; three blue stars above a heart, James Douglas's Coat of Arms, to which his descendants added a symbol of Bruce's heart. Possible salvation! I walked hesitantly into the Douglas Arms, steeling myself for more abuse or being ejected because of the dog. The opposite happened. Meg and I were welcomed in by both staff and punters. Comfortable in my own skin at last, I sat with a drink and a snack and charged my phone. The barman came over for a chat and fed Meg some biscuits. On the TV, the weatherman was explaining that the Saharan Dust that been blown over Britain in the last few days was still causing problems. The barman confirmed that his newly washed car had been covered in dust that morning. No way, man! I had always wanted to walk through the sands of the Sahara and here I was doing it in exclusive Bothwell. When the light faded, I snuck out and headed into the woods below Bothwell Castle, where I camped just out of sight of the local bourgeoisie.

In 1307, as he headed north, Bruce passed by the grand castle. It would have taken far more time, money and soldiers than he had available to crack this mighty fortress. I was forced to do the same. It was 8am when I arrived and raining heavily. The castle wouldn't be open for an hour and a half and I wasn't hanging around to get soaked. I circled the perimeter and carried on up the Clyde.

The River Clyde Way, total length 65km from New Lanark to Partick, was my passage into Glasgow and I followed the city's lifeblood into Uddingston before the path went pleasantly rural once more. Meg caused a commotion at Morrisons Supermarket near Cambuslang. I left her outside the entrance door whilst I nipped inside to use the toilet and buy a cup of coffee. When I returned, her lead was caught under the door and she was sitting on the pressure pad that activated the opening mechanism. She couldn't move, the door was opening and closing continually and animal-loving customers were looking furiously for the owner. Luckily, with all my waterproofs on and all the stuff – maps, hat, gloves, phone, wallet, camera, dictaphone, etc – that I had tucked inside my jacket giving me the physique of a Sumo wrestler, nobody gave me any serious trouble. Meg was fine and as I walked out into the torrential rain, smiling at my escape, I remembered a *Broons* cartoon that captured my unintended impersonation perfectly.

Daphne brings home a tall, athletic, dark haired, handsome man for a Hallowe'en party. The family are very impressed. Paw Broon offers to take the man's jacket; turns out, the jacket had giant shoulder pads; the fella is super skinny. To play the party games the man removes his giant platform heels (which had been hidden under his flares). Instead of being six foot tall, the man is nearer to five foot now. Playing catch the treacle scone (on a string) the sticky bun gets stuck in his hair and whips off the wig; the fella is as totally bald. To complete the man's ignominy, his false teeth got stuck in one of the apples that he was dooking for. He had a mouth like a newborn baby. I can't remember if the guy's personality won Daphne over in the end!

When I couldn't lift my head for the lashing rain, this was the kind of thing that my brain dredged up to keep me going. People must have seen me laughing away to myself. They must have though: that dog tells a good joke. Without Meg, I'd have been locked up more times than the naked rambler.

Crossing the Cambuslang Bridge, the urban cityscape eventually began to grow and familiar landmarks appeared. I passed the flat-roofed (Why? It's Scotland!) Commonwealth Games village near

A new bridge is lowered over the River Clyde.

Parkhead (after the Games, converted into 1,440 houses), and continued on under a freshly painted and now very attractive railway bridge at Dalmarnock. Next up, a fantastic site to watch, a brand new £5 million pedestrian bridge was being lowered into place, connecting Dalmarnock and Shawfield.

Into Britain's oldest public park, Glasgow Green, I marched, having followed the excellent signage along the riverside path highlighting distance, timing and points of interest. On 'The Green' is the People's Palace, a museum dedicated to the people of Glasgow and a 44m obelisk dedicated to the naval hero Viscount Horatio Nelson. James Watt, who arguably kick-started the industrial revolution, improved the steam engine using an idea he got walking in Glasgow Green. Of particular interest to me was that Bonnie Prince Charlie's army had camped here in 1745, on which occasion Charlie demanded shoes for his army from the city's cobblers. Given the continued bother I was having with my own feet, it was unfortunate that they hadn't left any behind.

I continued through Glasgow's more recent history, the Saltmarket, Glasgow Cross, the Trongate and Argyle Street. I was heading to a safe house in the city, a place where a manky walker could make himself respectable, empty his trash, clear the slugs from his dishes and collect a bag of 'I'm sick of pasta and porridge already' provisions. My friend Jennifer provided asylum. Later, we walked to Glasgow Cathedral, Scotland's finest surviving building from the 13th century, according to its guardian, Historic Scotland. It was the only cathedral in mainland Scotland to survive the Reformation period with its roof intact, due to the fact that the people of Glasgow agreed to pay for its upkeep. Dominated by its central tower, a later addition after the previous tower was destroyed in a lightning strike, this imposing gothic masterpiece was where Bruce headed in 1306, immediately after the murder of John Comyn.

Bishop Wishart of Glasgow had been a leading statesman of the country's fight for survival since the death of Alexander III in 1286. Throughout the period his name and actions stand out as a beacon of defiance against Plantagenet aggression. Famously, he stood up to Edward I's claims of overlordship in 1291 when as Guardian he stated 'the Scottish kingdom is not held in tribute or homage to anyone save God alone'.[11] Wishart also played an important role in instigating Wallace's rising of 1297, the zenith of which was the victory at Stirling Bridge. The Bishop was also a realist. Like Bruce, during the period 1297–1305 when the tide of fortune was turning inexorably against the Scots, he made peace with Edward in order to be able to live to fight another day. He was a believer in reviving the kingdom of Scotland above all else. With the fate of Scotland hanging in the balance, Wishart absolved Bruce of the murder of John Comyn and 'encouraged his flock to fight for Bruce as though his cause were a crusade'.[12] It may be that Bruce sought advice as well as absolution from Bishop Wishart. The Bishop's message was clear enough; he provided Robert with coronation robes and a royal banner which were hidden in the cathedral. This man was a giant, a titan of Scotland's struggle. His stature, given his age, experience and position, would have been above that of all others on the patriots' side. Who would argue against a man who for a full 20 years had been at the forefront of Scotland's struggle with Edward I? He was a man of his time, however, and his ideas on warfare were typical for the period. He used timber meant for his cathedral to build siege engines to attack castles, which he then occupied. I just wonder whether his influence on Bruce would have been overbearing. An English chronicler in 1306 called Wishart Bruce's chief adviser. Would a relatively young Bruce, aged 32, have the resolve or be strong enough, to argue against this man?

Sticking with 1306 and the time of Comyn's murder – Wishart played an active part in Bruce's coronation and brief attempt at seizing control of the country, prior to defeat at the battle of Methven. The Bishop was captured in one of the castles which he himself had just captured. It is possible that, free of the influence of elder statesmen such as Wishart whose successes were mixed, Bruce was able to come up with his own strategy for warfare and statesmanship, which he used so successfully on his return in 1307. At this juncture he was the senior man, with a younger band of lieutenants around him, and the force of resistance that he built was his and his alone. The confidence gained from doing this must have laid the foundations for Robert the Bruce to become the tactical genius that he most certainly was by 1314.

I headed inside the cathedral. Wishart aside, the Scottish Church played a critical role in maintaining Scotland's struggle for independence. The support of its leaders, the guidance it provided to ordinary people, its financial assistance, the learnedness of its bureaucrats and its contact with Rome (who regarded the Scottish Church as its 'special daughter') were all factors in Scotland's survival. Senior Scottish churchmen didn't want the hegemony of the Archbishops of York and the best way to avoid this was an independent Scotland.

Within the 13th-century crypt is the tomb of the battling Bishop, his headless effigy having partially survived the desecration of the Reformation; for a time it was confused with that of St Mungo, the founder of Glasgow, whose death in the 7th century led to the founding of a church upon the site of which the cathedral now stands. My visit was cut short when the fire alarm sounded. When it was clear there wasn't going to be a disastrous spectacle, Jen led me through a maze

The tomb of Bishop Wishart in the crypt of Glasgow Cathedral.

of city centre streets, under the M8 motorway and up to the Forth and Clyde Canal, heading towards Maryhill. The weather had improved markedly and I hung my tent on the back of my rucksack to dry, as I did most days. We walked along the towpath chatting and I aired a few regrets and hang-ups. Should have, could have, and might have? Pointless dwelling on the past, I know – another symptom of spending a long time on your own. I had known Jen since childhood and she knew the background to my complaints. I had been storing them up for a little bit, but Jen swatted away my moans in with a giant bat of positivity and by the time we went our separate ways I felt a lot better. It's good to talk.

At Maryhill the canal descends via five lock gates, the 'Maryhill Steps', down to the Kelvin Aqueduct, the longest in Europe in its heyday. We left the canal at this point, descended from the aqueduct and followed the River Kelvin Walkway. The signposts got confusing as we walked up to Maryhill Road and then on into Summerston before going down by John Paul Academy, towards the river once more. Jen took her leave at this point and ran back into the city centre. She had been really encouraging and I had exorcised a few ghosts from the past.

Walking along the mucky river bank, I didn't realise that the tent, still drying on my back, was trailing through the sludge! By the time I noticed, a large part of my accommodation was absolutely clarty. I laid it out in a field to give it a good clean, cursing my carelessness, time wasted, effort required, blah de blah! Then I bloody realised I hadn't left enough water left for my evening meal, so I had to take a chance on taking it from the Kelvin. At the riverbank there was an oily substance leaking from an old drum, so I tried a little further upstream. Thereafter, I used half a canister of gas boiling the hell out of it, still cursing to myself.

I awoke a bit groggy from my big walk the previous day, or had I poisoned myself? I had been in such a deep sleep that I hadn't even wakened when one end of the tent collapsed on top of me during the night. After over two weeks of continuous walking, I was ready for a day off. Calling my daughter Kara and wishing her a happy 13th birthday was both happy and painful for me. I needed regular pauses in my conversation in order not to start blubbing. Once I started, I might never have stopped. I had left a card for her which I could tell was appreciated. All seemed well on the home front also, which was reassuring, and Nicola told me she had managed to book a bunkhouse for me in Balmaha. All lethargy forgotten, I was a man on a mission. Operation 'Head for a Bed in Balmaha' began. Continuing with the River Kelvin Way, I reached the Balmuildy Bridge and took a shortcut along the A739. It was pavement all the way until I rejoined the riverside path. Soon there was a golf club on my left and Murray Park Football Academy on my right. It was 9am, golfers were out; footballers were still in bed and every time I looked at the river and saw all the trash in it, my stomach heaved. I crossed the Kelvin once again at the Prescott Bridge and chatted to a local man who guided me on into Milngavie, the official start of the West Highland Way, my route north.

As I headed for the toilet, a chap setting up the Caurnie Soaperie stall for the weekly farmers' market asked if I was all set for my walk. He

A delicious treat from the Queen of Hearts.

had read about our previous adventure and in particular remembered about the sores that Meg had suffered from – it's always the bloody dog that steals the show! Jim gave me a bottle of germanium body wash (hint, hint!) and introduced Meg and me to other stallholders. For our journey we were given cakes, pies and Kirsten from Queen of Hearts, Cakes & Tarts gave us some harlequin slice, a favourite of mine and a recipe that I thought was exclusive to my own family. Going into a shop to buy some water, I came out to find that Meg was getting her photo taken with a fan of border collies. What a fantastic and uplifting hour!

Feeling on top of the world (my gut rot must have been paranoia), I got started on the West Highland Way, following the Allander Water to Drumclog Moor and then travelling on into Mugdock Wood. There was a flow of walkers on the paths and I seemed to have started at the back of the grid. I focused on the next group ahead and reeled them in. It was a perfect day for walking; under a bright sky, the air was cool and still and the West Highland Way endeared rapidly itself to me. After exiting the woods, it felt like I had stepped into a different world. I found myself in a rural setting overlooking Craigallan Loch. Memories came flooding back of having walked this way three years previously with my eldest daughter, Sophie, who was only 11 at the time. Walking the entire West Highland Way, she had coped remarkably well, but I had been carrying for two and the thought of the weight of that rucksack brought tears to my eyes. Soon, I was walking along the Blane valley at the foot of the Campsie Hills, with a volcanic plug, Dumgoyne, ahead. Continuing along the route of a disused railway, I bypassed Killearn in the company of a German student called Carsten, talking about football, a pretty universal topic that I find never goes wrong.

In the village of Drymen I met a couple of Dutch guys walking the 'Highland Highway'. Thinking myself a fount of knowledge on two-footed Scottish journeys, I was flummoxed. 'Tell me more?' I asked. It was, they explained a high-level version of the West Highland Way, taking in a lot of summits, including 23 Munros.

I stopped for a drink at the Clachan Inn, the oldest licensed premises in Scotland (1734). Given that I hadn't had a decent wash for a fortnight, I sat at the far corner of the pub, well away from everyone else, and shouted pleasantries across the room.

The roadside from Drymen to Balmaha was pavement all the way.

On the West Highland Way. Dumgoyne ahead and little Dumgoyach on the left.

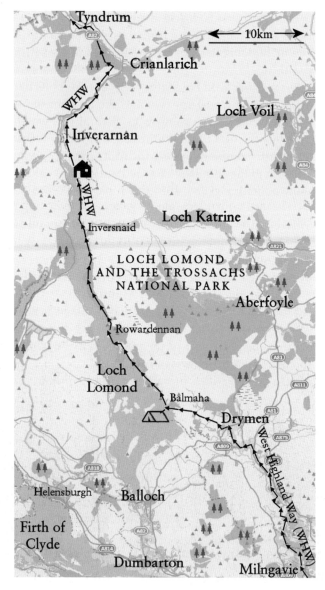

The West Highland Way.

Near to the little tourist village and yachting centre, I got my first stunning views of Loch Lomond. I turned up at the bunkhouse run by Jock, who barked out the rules and then left me to the luxury of a large living room/kitchen, bathroom and dormitory. I didn't feel guilty about spending a night under a roof; I couldn't have camped in the area, as between March and October there is a no wild camping rule in this part of the Loch Lomond and Trossachs National Park. I don't think Nicola would have booked me in here if she had known the sleeping arrangements – the only other occupant of the room was a German student, Arianna, whose boyfriend was in New Zealand.

The next day was a rest day, thankfully. My weary body certainly needed the rest. I met up with my pal Graeme, who pulled up his car at MacFarlane's Boatyard and together we proceeded to pull shedloads of gear out of the boot. Every eventuality looked as if it had been covered by my thorough companion.

A small passenger launch, which doubled as the mail boat for Loch Lomond's islands, took us over to Inchcailloch Island, just a short distance from Balmaha. There is a tenuous link with Robert the Bruce, who is credited with introducing roe deer to the islands of

Quality camping with Graeme at Inchcailloch Island.

Loch Lomond; the deer in these royal hunting forests would be safe from predators, including wolves. Six hundred years before The Bruce, an Irish saint, St Kentigerna, lived on the island. In 1903, a skeleton believed to be hers was found under a slab of white sandstone within the ruins of the medieval church.

There was an official campsite on the now uninhabited island and we would be the first overnight visitors of the year. We had to get there first though; I struggled uphill from the tiny pier, carrying my rucksack, a bag of coal and a huge stove. Graeme was equally encumbered. A 20-minute stagger got us to Port Bawn on the southwest of the island. Then it was back to the pier for a second lot of equipment. The campsite was a little island paradise: a sheltered bay with a sandy beach overlooking a tiny islet, Torrinch. The facilities were ample: a large fire pit and a composting toilet.

We put up our tents right away and Graeme set up his kitchen at a picnic bench. It was marvellous sitting round a big fire, eating, chatting and relaxing, whilst looking out over the little bay. The weather was overcast but dry and at this time of year the island was midge free. Meg hardly moved an inch, unless required; she lay flat out, recuperating.

Later in the afternoon, we walked through oak woodland up to the ruins of the 13th-century church and graveyard. Highland funerals were hard-drinking affairs; in folklore there are tales of bodies being lost en route to the cemetery and even of mourners forgetting to bury the dead. Edicts and laws were passed in 1645 and 1701 to curb the excessive consumption, but even in the present day, the drinking goes on unabated. As Graeme and I approached the graveyard, a wooden coffin lay forgotten on a wall.

My companion kept his *pièce de résistance* until early evening when he cooked a couple of sirloin steaks with onions and vegetables, accompanied by baked potatoes from the fire. Condiments were mustard or brown sauce. After a fortnight of dried foods, the taste, texture and juiciness was mindblowing. I knew he was a bit of a Keith Floyd and had heard stories of his family soup competitions, but this was something else. Any misgivings about the amount of gear he had brought had been erased hours ago, but this was a new high in

Alongside Loch Lomond on the West Highland Way.

campfire cuisine. I was moved by his efforts. Royal hunting forest or not Bruce never ate this well.

The following morning, Sandy picked us up as arranged at 9.30am and we motored back over to the mainland. To our relief, he explained that the coffin had been left behind after a theatrical re-enactment the previous year. I took leave of Graeme and thanked him for everything he had done to make it a memorable day off. Over the last seven days, I had had support from George, Jennifer and Graeme. Their enthusiasm provided me with more inner strength and determination. I owed it to them as well as to my loving, deserted family to make sure I did my utmost to complete the journey, which had almost overwhelmed me at the outset, but was fast becoming manageable, both physically and mentally.

I continued along the shore of Loch Lomond, following Bruce as he headed north. Scotland's largest and best known loch is surrounded by natural beauty and steeped in the history of the clans, who lived, loved and lost here. I love the phrase describing what the loch was once famed for: 'Waves without wind, fish without fin and a floating island.' A swell on the widest part of the loch after a storm caused the first anomaly. The second was a type of snake that swam between some of the loch's 49 islands and islets. The third curiosity must have been man-made, possibly a crannog.[13] Although I couldn't know the exact route that Bruce took, it would have been to the east of the loch, similar to the route of the West Highland Way, as this land belonged to his supporter the Earl of Lennox, whereas on the west side, enemies lurked.

Soon I was looking out across the water to Inchlonaig Island, which was planted with yew trees on the orders of Robert the Bruce. Yew trees supplied the wood for longbows which English and Welsh archers used to devastating effect in wars against the Scots and the French. Forward-thinking Bruce was trying to help the Scots of future generations compete in archery battles. At Rowardennan, a stopping point for 18th-century cattle drovers, the public road terminates and nowadays is a stopping point for Munro baggers' cars as the climbers take the footpath for Ben Lomond. I had made 'never miss a toilet' my war cry and there were decent facilities here. Having made good progress so far, the next leg to Inversnaid reduced my pace considerably. To start with, the forest road was fairly undulating, as was the narrow track which followed on from it. When the track headed down to the rocky shore, the walking was more awkward and slower, frustrating me, as I was impatient to reach the Inversnaid Hotel. Seventeen days after my previous visit, I duly returned; I stopped for a drink and was delighted with to be served with a whole cafetiere of coffee and a jug of milk.

Possibly the caffeine enthused me unnaturally, but I really enjoyed the next section of the route to the northern tip of Loch Lomond. The narrow and rocky shore-hugging path required concentration, but walking with sticks gave me four points of contact and the resultant stability had me flying along. I remembered struggling along this section on my previous trip with my daughter so I was delighted to be making such good progress as I neared the end of a long day. At the head of the loch, a herd of feral goats were sharing a grassy meadow with a herd of red deer. Meg stayed where she was and I tip-toed towards them, marvelling at my good fortune. The goats of Loch Lomond are said to have a connection with Robert the Bruce: a herd of these hardy grazers

The wild goats of Loch Lomondside.

lay in front of the entrance to a cave in which he was sheltering whilst a fugitive, giving him protection from his enemies and the elements. Bruce, always one to reward those who helped him, enacted a law to exempt goats from grassmail, the method by which tenant farmers paid rent.[14]

After taking a few photographs I patted my pockets looking for my dictaphone, intending to record a few thoughts. With increasing frenzy I patted away, but the familiar shape wasn't there. Panicking, I turned out each of my pockets but to no avail; I must have dropped the damned thing. With over 200 comments on it I couldn't afford to lose it. I looked around the immediate vicinity but it wasn't there. I would have to retrace my steps. The best of moments had turned into the worst of moments. With all thoughts of wildlife forgotten, I put down all my gear and ran back from whence I had come. Sustained by the adrenalin pumping hard through my body, I berated myself for not zipping up my pockets properly. After 20 minutes, my sanity was saved. I saw the little black case lying on the path, a little mucky but otherwise none the worse for wear. Turning around, I jogged back towards the head of the loch again and by early evening I reached Doune Bothy. Relieved that there was mobile phone coverage, I phoned Nicola; it was our wedding anniversary. She had secretly shoved a card into my rucksack before leaving, which I put above the fireplace. Thereafter, I had a night away from the elements in front of a roasting fire in a converted byre, but having heard everyone's voices the bothy seemed quiet and lifeless. I stared into the flames and thought of happy times.

I wasn't brimming with enthusiasm the next day and the low motivation induced a desire to linger longer at rest stops and viewpoints. At mid-morning, I was looking across the River Falloch. High on the other side of the valley, I could see the Stone of the Britons – an ancient marker of the territorial border between the Britons of Strathclyde and the Scots of Dalriada. Under these stones Bruce was reputed to have spent an evening during his fugitive days. I had lunch at a picnic bench on the top of a steep slope above Crianlarich, where Glen Falloch meets Strath Fillan, and welcomed other breathless walkers to the mini-summit with the dubious smell of curried noodles. Retracing my steps of almost three weeks previously, I walked north past the remains of Strathfillan Priory and Dalrigh to the village of Tyndrum.

To say I was in something of a sweat that evening would be an understatement; a nervous wreck would be more apt. I was due to spend the following day walking with a reporter, Garry, from the *Scots Magazine*, but my route plan was looking a bit harum-scarum. The idea was to follow a footpath from Tyndrum down Glen Cononish until Ben Lui, one of the southern Highlands' most popular and iconic mountains, was towering over us. Then we would walk round the mountain in an anticlockwise direction, passing over a 430m bealach before descending through a forestry plantation into Glen Lochy. From there we would cross the River Lochy and march along an old military road through more forest, before exiting onto the main road and following this into Dalmally. Finally, we would walk along a back road into Loch Awe village.

It was a hell of a proposition and I hoped Garry was a hill man and reasonably fit. We couldn't be late into Loch Awe, or he would miss the last train back to Tyndrum. The plan to walk through the forest was dodgy, as the path didn't show up on my 1:50,000 map, only on the more detailed 1:25000 Explorer map. From previous experience of forestry plantations, I reckoned there was little chance of this path being any use – and without paths, forestry plantations were impenetrable barriers. Thirdly, I realised that there was no bridge where I planned to cross the River Lochy; it was a ford, which I found out by a bit of last-ditch internet research to be uncrossable in spate conditions. With the recent weather it was definitely going to be spate conditions. On top of which, walking along the A85 could be dangerous, or at best very slow, depending how busy the road and how wide the verges. I was terrified of the walk being a disaster and the reporter would have every right to go to town on me, either personally, or in the written press. My butterflies must have transferred themselves to the dog because her guts rumbled terribly during the night and the reek was hazardous. Getting up several times during the night to let her out to the toilet and to get a bit of fresh air myself was a price worth paying. The alternative was unthinkable.

CHAPTER 4

Argyll

I MET WITH Garry at Lower Tyndrum Station, one of the village's two railway stations. My first worry about whether he was a hill man was soothed as I approached the car park and saw him in proper hillwalking gear (not brand new of course, that *would* have been a concern). We walked through the forest on the west side of Strathfillan, into Glen Cononish, and it turned out my worries were completely unfounded, as Garry was a lot more experienced on the hills than me. He had been all over the country with the *Scots Magazine* and ran a hillwalking club.

We were leaving Stirlingshire and heading into Argyll, following Bruce as he took on his enemies the MacDougalls. They were the masters of the western seaboard, loyal to Balliol and now in league with the King of England. They were one of three key enemies whom Bruce would have to defeat if he was to make himself master of Scotland. Already they had inflicted defeat upon Bruce in 1306 at the Battle of Dalrigh, where I had started my journey three weeks before.

Normally Glen Cononish is a lovely walk, but it was a wet, windy and misty morning. Chatting with Gary passed the time admirably and before long we were at the end of the track, where only the lower slopes of Ben Lui were visible in front of us. We walked round the mountain rather than going over it, and over slippery ground we traced a line of old fence posts gently uphill to a rounded bealach between a northern spur of Ben Lui and Beinn Chuirn.

With the wind now slamming into us, we lingered not and immediately started purposefully downhill. Ahead, on the lower slopes of the mountain, I could see the Eas Daimh River, draining the slopes of Ben Lui and Beinn Dubh and disappearing into the forestry plantation. If the path through the forest was overgrown, as I feared, then hopefully, we could still follow the course of the river into Glen Lochy.

At the edge of the plantation, the first obstacle was a 2m deer fence.

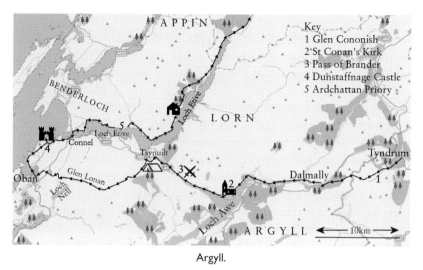

Argyll.

Seeing no gates or styles nearby Garry climbed over first and was able to receive a none too happy dog. There was indeed a faint path by the northern bank of the Eas Daimh; the ground was saturated, but we were already soaked through, so we plodded on undeterred. Out of the blue, we came to a spanking new bridge and forestry road. Garry was keen on following this and I was quite happy to be led for a change. We crossed the river and headed along the new road. The good going underfoot was spoiled by the nagging worry of following a road whose destination we did not know. After a short distance, uncertainty got the better of us and we hurried back to the river, where the path was now on the unreachable far bank. We negotiated our way downstream anyway, pushing our way through the trees, which were perched close to and sometimes overhanging the bank. Eventually, frustratingly close to the forest edge, we reached an impenetrable barrier of fallen pines. Retracing our steps back up the river, we turned away from the roaring waters and fought our way through the plantation to try and circumvent the area of devastation. This was hard going with every branch trying its best to impede our progress. We won through to a cleared section of forest where we still had the rigmarole of another *three* full height deer fences to negotiate before we were free. Breathless but relieved, we nipped over the railway to reach the confluence of the Eas Daimh and River Lochy, just upstream of which was the ford over the Lochy. Seeing the speed of the water, we both agreed there was no way we could get across this safely, even though we could hardly get any wetter; a bridge, one kilometre away would suffice. Already feeling the strain of a tough morning in tough conditions, following the river pushed us to our limits. The boggy ground and numerous tributaries took their toll on our already depleted energy reserves and morale. After crossing the river at the footbridge, we were at the point where we really needed some shelter and rest. Thankfully, we found a little spot out of the wind and the rain where hot food and coffee restored my spirits and Garry sang the praises of his landlady who had made him a hearty packed lunch. Meg seemed untroubled as usual.

The A85 runs alongside the River Lochy, down the glen of the same name, connecting Tyndrum with Oban. We followed it for seven kilometres to the village of Dalmally. The first hour was fine as we strode purposefully along the quiet road and nattered about football. Then the rain fell once more, the heaviest downpour I had experienced on the journey so far. Garry and I planned on going to Loch Awe together, but when we reached Dalmally, he said that was far enough for the day, shook my hand and walked off into the nearest hotel; he returned quickly enough – it was residents only. Further into the village we came to the Glen Orchy Lodge Hotel. I went into the welcoming bar with him to escape the torrential rain; we left our dripping waterproofs at the front door, where they created an enormous slipping hazard. Even with the outer layers shed, my inner layers were soaked through with sweat; plus, walking with sticks had caused water to run up my sleeves, soaking further my fleece jacket and base layer. Leaning on the bar for support, Garry said it was his hardest day in the hills for a while! After a civilised coffee and a short rest, I knew I had to push on. I left Garry by the roadside, as he tried to thumb a lift back to Tyndrum. If the worst came to the worst, he could catch a train a couple of hours hence. I was grateful that yet again, during awful conditions, I had the pleasure of company to help me see it through. Amazingly, the weather did a complete turnaround – the rain stopped, the wind dropped and

Loch Awe narrowing to the Pass of Brander ahead.

the clouds cleared. I decided to walk myself dry. Still following the main road, I came round by Loch Awe, at 41km the longest freshwater loch in Scotland. Here at the eastern edge was a calendar favourite, the ever-watchful ruins of 15th-century Kilchurn Castle, one-time home of the Campbells of Glen Orchy. Reaching Lochawe village just before 5pm, I went into the local grocers for a newspaper and asked about the cairn devoted to Robert the Bruce, supposedly near the railway station. The lady knew nothing of it, but did tell me that one of Bruce's bones was in the local church. I was gobsmacked. How did I not know about this? I had a good look around the train station for the cairn, which I didn't see any sign of, although I liked the railway carriage holiday home, parked right beside the station, overlooking the loch. I hurried on to St Conan's Kirk.

In this remote location, inside a remarkable church that clings to the steep hillside, is a chapel containing an effigy of Robert the Bruce. The early evening light shining through the 15th-century window onto the alabaster hands and face brought a realistic, deathly pallor to the King's face. Below the body was an ossuary containing a toe bone of the King. In the presence of the resting monarch, it seemed the right place to whisper a short prayer, or maybe begin a Q&A session. In my mind, Bruce was still alive and well, and at the head of an army marching towards the Pass of Brander.

I hurried along the narrow main road and at Innis Chonain, where the A85 crossed the railway line on a narrow bridge, there was ongoing maintenance work and no pavement. I squeezed between a protective barrier and the wall of the road bridge only to find myself walking atop plastic pipes. Stumbling, I let go of Meg's lead, nearly killing my companion, as she instantly sought easier ground under the barrier, bringing an oncoming car to a nose-diving halt. A guilty wave and an awkward smile to the driver, and I went quickly on my way. I was shaken; Meg wasn't stirred. Hundreds and hundreds of miles I had walked with her and that was the closest I had come to losing her. It wasn't just the dog I'd have lost; I'd been warned that if I didn't come home with the family pet then I wasn't to come home at all!

The narrow Pass of Brander, squeezed between Loch Awe and giant Ben Cruachan, allows access to Oban and the west coast. Before reaching the narrowest, steepest section of the pass, I stopped and ate at a picnic bench at the Ben Cruachan visitor centre: 50,000 people a year enter the hollowed-out mountain, which contains a hydroelectric power station capable of generating 440,000,000 watts of electricity, enough to power 350,000 homes! A notice board told the tale of the battle, which took place 2km further along the road, where the pass was at its narrowest. Robert the Bruce was coming into Argyll to attack the MacDougalls, the Lords of Lorne, and the most powerful force on the western seaboard of Scotland: 'all the garrisons from Dingwall in the Ross to the Mull of Kintyre were in their possession.'[15]

Alexander, the chief, was married to a Comyn and nailed his colours to that mast. The seat of their power was Dunstaffnage Castle, a mighty fortress to the north of Oban. A formidable enemy at the peak of their powers. Alexander's son John had already defeated Bruce at the Battle of Dalrigh, hunted him in Galloway and now hoped to ambush the King here at the Pass of Brander. Alas for John, Robert foresaw the trap. The King's party advanced along the narrow path while the MacDougalls lay hidden on the slopes above, ready to charge down

The curtain wall of Dunstaffnage Castle, virtually unchanged since it was built in the 13th century.

upon the King's men as they passed underneath. Bruce, however, had read the ground well and at the site of St Conan's Church he had sent a detachment of Highlanders commanded by James Douglas to swarm high up the slopes of Ben Cruachan, beyond where he anticipated the trap to be set. When Bruce's army reached the noose of the trap, they charged uphill. Douglas's men shot arrows upon the MacDougalls and charged downhill. Caught in a pincer movement, John MacDougall's men were routed and fled back towards the bridge over the River Awe, which they intended to destroy. They never got the chance. The King's men were on their heels and they secured the bridgehead before pursuing the MacDougalls all the way back to Dunstaffnage Castle.

The Pass of Brander, still the main route to Oban from central Scotland, now supports a railway line as well as a road. The visitor centre protrudes into the loch somewhat and I could see that the road ahead was built overhanging the loch, supported by stilts. I marched on into the narrow defile; steep-sided, mountainous flanks to my right, Loch Awe, narrowing to the River Awe on my left. Unfortunately for me, the pavement came to an end. It was now a deadly game of avoiding hurtling traffic on blind corners, sharp bends and chicanes; treading gingerly, eyes and ears alert for the sounds of approaching vehicles. Some sections were so narrow and steep that there was nowhere to get off the road, so I jogged those parts. All thoughts of the battle were forgotten as I made my way through the pass. The only thing in my favour was timing: it was Sunday evening and the road was at its quietest. Reaching the Loch Awe Barrage (another hydroelectric scheme), I had passed the worst – and the battle site! I got off road by following a well-built fisherman's path along the River Awe where there was even a steel footbridge over sections of otherwise impassable rock.

It was dusk by the time I reached Bridge of Awe village and without any armed resistance I crossed River Awe. Looking to my left, I could see the ruined remains of the previous road bridge where one arch of the original three still stood. Built in 1779, it lasted until 1990 when it was destroyed – by floods, not MacDougalls. I followed the main road once more and camped on the outskirts of Taynuilt, exhausted but dry.

It was a lovely, gently warming spring morning as I walked through peaceful Glen Lonan – the 'Road of Kings'.[16] This was part of the ancient procession route taken by the lifeless bodies of Scottish Kings one thousand years ago as they were borne to their final resting place: the Isle of Iona. Walking along the valley floor past farms, open fields, and pasture, where Highland cattle roamed freely – but at a distance – was a real pleasure. To the north was Deadh Choimhead, which translates beautifully as 'keeper of the twilight'. Under this hill, a natural fortress with its terraces of rocky knolls, I had a late breakfast on my own little knoll protruding from the soft floor of the glen. Ahead lay a shallow lochan, populated by herons and black-throated divers. A calling cuckoo was my background music as I rejoiced in my freedom.

It wasn't just unspoiled natural beauty: the sites of ancient settlements were evident along the way and looking over to the crannogs of Loch Nell was Clach na Carraig, a roughly cut standing stone, 3.8 metres high – said to mark the grave of Diarmaid, an Irish hero. At the end of the glen I continued west; Kenneth MacAlpin, Macbeth *et al* would have been taken south, past Loch Nell to Loch Feochan, where their cortege would have set sail for Iona. Descending gently from Glen Cruitten, I reached Oban, the gateway to the Isles of Scotland, the town was a lot quieter than on my previous visit, when the harbour area was thronged with people watching the antics of a sperm whale taking shelter in the bay. I passed underneath Dunollie Castle, a MacDougall stronghold built on an imposing rock promontory, guarding Oban bay and the sound of Kerrera. There remains a four-storey tower camouflaged in ivy, which was at one time protected by a strong curtain wall. In Bruce's time the chief seat of Clan MacDougall, the Lords of Lorne was nearby Dunstaffnage Castle. The fate of the occupants of this stronghold during Bruce's incursion is unknown.

Dunollie still belongs to the MacDougalls and the family of the chiefs reside in a more modern edifice nearby. The famous Brooch of Lorn, is also retained by the MacDougalls, where it is held for safe keeping in an Oban bank vault. It was reputed to have adorned Robert the Bruce before being snatched from his clothing at the Battle of Dalrigh, which makes clear how close to capture the King was. Subsequently, the brooch has been dated to the 16th-century, although the charm stone contained within may well have belonged to the Bruce.

I ended the day just past the sandy beach of Ganavan Bay, where from my tent door I could look over to the opposing chessboard rooks of Maclean's Duart Castle on the Isle of Mull and Robert Stevenson's lighthouse on Eilean Musdile.

Four kilometres north of Oban, built on a rocky outcrop, on a promontory at the mouth of Loch Etive, stands majestic 13th-century Dunstaffnage Castle, virtually unchanged since Bruce's attack. Taking its shape from the rock, the high curtain wall was interspersed with three rounded towers. Only arrow slits, subsequently widened to gun holes, pierce this formidable 18m high defensive ring where the walls were up to 3.5m thick. A magnificent stronghold for the Lords of Lorne, the senior descendants of Somerled, the undisputed King of the Isles. In my copy of Barbour's *Bruce,* edited by AAM Duncan, there is a description of Bruce's attack:

> The King that stout wes sark and bauld,
> Till Dunstaffynch ryscht sturdely,

A sege set and besily
Assaylit the castell it to get
And in schort tym he has thaim set
In swilk thrang that tharin war than
That magre tharis he it wan...

The King who was strong, firm and bold,
Went to Dunstaffnage,
A sturdy and diligent siege was set,
The castle was assailed,
In a short time he has them densely packed inside
And in spite of these men he won it.

Although his son John escaped, Alexander, the MacDougall chief, submitted to Bruce, attending a parliament in 1309 at St Andrews. By nullifying the threat of the powerful MacDougalls, one of his three key Scottish enemies, Bruce had also secured his western seaboard; Communication with Ireland could be established and his allies including Angus Og MacDonald and Neil Campbell, whose lands were on this coastline and the surrounding islands, would be better able to support him. Furthermore, the forces of Edward II would be less able to turn Bruce's flank, giving the King one less reason to look over his shoulder when he turned to face his southern adversaries.

I climbed the steps of the 16th-century gatehouse, virtually the only change to the castle's defences since Bruce's time. This was one of only a few fortresses that, despite being captured by the King, was not destroyed, but instead kept as a centre of royal power in the area. Quite possibly this was intended as a royal castle anyway, such was its strength, built at the expense of King Alexander III and maintained by the MacDougalls on behalf of the King. I walked along the airy top of the thick curtain wall, imagining Bruce's satisfaction at the turnaround in fortunes and the bringing to heel of an enemy who had so nearly, and on more than one occasion, ended his kingship. Revenge was not served on the leading members of the family however; Bruce's political

The remains of Ardchattan Priory. Bruce met the West Highland chiefs here.

savvy was demonstrated as he made peace with Alexander.

For my next objective, Ardchattan Priory, I had no choice but to follow the busy A85 to Connell at the mouth of Loch Etive; here, where the loch is at its narrowest, a spectacular cantilever bridge crossing the tidal narrows was built in 1905. It carried only rail traffic until a road was built alongside the tracks; in 1965, the road users finally got the bridge to themselves with the demise of the Ballachulish to Oban railway branch. On the north side, accompanying the great sea loch inland, I made my way east towards Ardchattan Priory.

Having reduced the power of the MacDougalls, Bruce had a meeting with local chiefs at the 13th-century priory, traditionally held to be the last parliament in which Gaelic was the dominant tongue. In the 21st century, Latin was the dominant tongue in the fine gardens. There is little left of the priory buildings. In the 16th century, much of the church was dismantled to provide materials for the construction of a dwelling house. I had lunch under a surviving double archway which once led from the choir to the transept.

Now I set out to catch up with Bruce as he made his way towards Inverlochy Castle at Fort William, which belonged to his chief rivals,

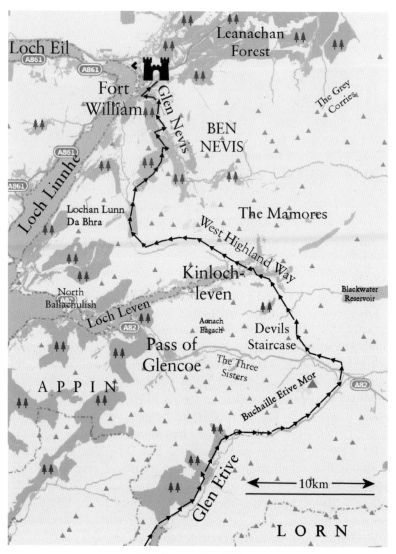

Glen Etive to Fort William.

the Comyns. I was going to continue alongside Loch Etive, to its head, 30 km inland. Glen Etive would lead me onto the Rannoch Moor, where I could rejoin the West Highland Way and follow it almost to its conclusion.

The terrain became more mountainous as the afternoon wore on. The hamlet of Bonawe, after which the nearby 18th-century iron furnace is named, was at the end of the road, where a right of way allows access through a working quarry. Passing under a disused face, the path then skirts round huge piles of gravel collected by oversized dumper trucks. On the hillside above, giant boulders were being pushed around by bulldozers. When the footpath returned me to the water's edge Ben Cruachan was once again towering above me, although this time we were separated by Loch Etive. I was in wild terrain, on my own once more and a familiar feeling struck me – a mixture of loneliness, apprehension and excitement. Meg at least was glad to be off-road and off the lead again. She roamed around tirelessly. I relaxed also and looked forward to a night under a fixed roof.

There was no chimney smoke as I approached Cadderlie bothy so I guessed I had it to myself. Other than that, I was delighted with what I found. The cottage, which is maintained by members of the Mountain Bothy Association, has three rooms: two living areas, each with its own fireplace, and a bedroom. The better furnished of the two living rooms contained a sofa, table, chairs, a drinks cabinet and a well-stocked library. It was clean, tidy and quite incredibly, I found it to be kitted out with a selection of fresh (and not so fresh) supplies. Food stocks included, milk and fresh pasta – still in date! There were also crisps, pot noodles, a tin of baked beans and a packet of cheesy macaroni. However, there were many other foodstuffs that were well past their best: fusty morning rolls; mouldy cheese; mouldy paté; soft oatcakes; brick-hard chocolate Rice Krispie cake. No wonder the visitors book mentioned a wee moose. I was only surprised it was 'wee' and not the size of a large dog. In the past, I have been grateful for the occasional packet or can of food left at a bothy, but to leave fresh food was just daft. There was also a large quantity of red wine that, thankfully, I didn't find until the following morning, otherwise the party could have got out of hand. In the end I had fresh pasta stuffed with ham and Parmesan cheese for dinner, served with cheese and onion crisps and milky coffee. I ate until it became painful and Meg thought she had died and had gone to heaven – such was the quality and quantity of her evening meal. Then a bonfire (of the profanities) in the fireplace as I burned all the nauseating food. The Rice Krispie Cake burned especially well, nearly setting the lum aflame. Selecting Stephen Fry's autobiography from the library, I relaxed within the hot, glowing room where the shadows danced on the back wall and only the furiously rattling windows gave any clue as to the goings-on outside.

The next morning it was a thought to leave, especially after I found the wine! Outside it was windy, murky and wet from the overnight deluge. The river by the bothy was roaring so loud that Meg was too frightened to come out the door. Back on the footpath, I was soon in the midst of a forestry plantation. Crossing the Allt Easach on a concrete bridge without side rails was dramatic and deafening; a sea of white water cascaded down the hillside, underneath my feet and then onwards. The rain must have washed away all the snow on the hilltops for there to have been such a huge volume of water. A track continued through the plantation above Loch Etive before the forest went native, reverting to birch, Scots pine and holly. In due course, the path headed down to follow the water's edge where stream after stream tumbled into the loch. I reached a small jetty near the head of the loch, used primarily to load felled timber onto boats – an environmentally friendly method for transporting the 250,000 tons of timber that requires harvesting in this glen.

Travelling by boat up the length of Loch Etive was for hundreds of years the main method of reaching Glen Etive, which would have made it seem far less remote than it seems now, from a motorist's perspective. I arrived at the head of the loch and joined the public road as it began to wind its way northeast along the glen, at one time the idyllic home of Deirdre of the Sorrows, a legendary Scots-Irish heroine. There was no dramatic scenery to report as my views were restricted within a corridor of rhododendrons and the cloud was just above head height. There was no sign of the Munros, which, according to my map, were surrounding me – just some steep hillsides disappearing quickly into the mist. I took an early lunch within a patch of conifers whilst a bulldozer worked nearby, pulling them from the ground, its grappling arm manoeuvring the trunks like a majorette twirling her baton. The River Etive, with its pools, falls and sections of rapids, was the intermittent focus of my attention during the long walk up the glen. I wimped out of taking a planned shortcut through the Lairig Gartain, the high pass between Buachaille Etive Mor and Buachaille Etive Beag: the amount of water streaming off the hillsides, the wind, rain and mist put me off climbing through that. Instead I took the longer, lower route following the road round the iconic Buachaille Etive Mor, the Herdsman; a bit monotonous in the conditions but safe, or so I thought. Two beautiful French girls stopped their car to offer me a lift. They said the dog looked sad. I didn't argue, I had been sad too until this point. I reluctantly refused and continued on the long road out of the glen. In depressing conditions, I switched on my phone and listened to a podcast which I had saved for emergencies; *Film Review* with Mark Kermode and Simon Mayo. One of the reviews was for *Under the Skin* starring Scarlett Johansson – a film set in Scotland, where an alien posing as a beautiful female stops to offer male pedestrians a lift in her car and then murders those who accept. Initially, according to Mark, some of the men didn't know they were being filmed! Look out for Meg and me in the French version! Happily riding along, Meg's head leaning out of the window of the car; me smiling in the back seat as the miles are eaten up, then, whoosh, melted into a pint of plasma. My imagination was going overboard, I know, but it was all I had to think about.

Finally, I emerged from Glen Etive and, reaching the A82 at the western edge of the Rannoch Moor, I crossed the road to get back onto the West Highland Way, just beyond the King's House Hotel. At the car park at nearby Altnafeadh, there was a joyful reunion with Nicola and the girls. Squeezed into the car with all my gear, getting respite from the weather, I sat with a pile of treats, catching up on their activities over the three and a bit weeks. In the boot, Meg was reunited with her sparring partner, our older collie, Ailsa. I was delighted with

Old Inverlochy Castle, a massive statement of Comyn power.

the news that my two elder daughters wanted to tackle the Devil's Staircase with me, although the wee one, Abbie, was disappointed she couldn't go too – someone had to keep Mum company. Sophie and Kara raced each other up the 250m ascent while I lagged well behind. Reaching the top of the pass, we walked and talked together, following the long path, an old military road through the hills downhill towards Kinlochleven, where I camped at the Black Mount Campsite. Nicola collected the girls and I arranged to meet them at Fort William where I was planning on a day off.

My outlook, often dominated by the weather, was bright as I began the 25th day of my journey. Climbing up towards the Lairig Mor, the Big Pass, there were good views west over to Loch Leven, from which emerged the steadily climbing, knobbly north ridges of both the Pap of Glencoe and snow-capped Sgorr Dhearg. Up on the pass, busy with walkers fore and aft, the colours on the hillsides were vibrant and welcoming. I bashed on, anxious to spend some more time with my family. At a distance I passed Lochan Lunn Da Bhra (for clarification, it doesn't mean upstanding cleavage), where Macbeth's crannog still breaks the surface of the water. Nearby a large cairn marks the spot where in 1645 the MacDonalds called a halt to their pursuit of the Campbells after the Battle of Inverlochy. This route was the main one in the 17th century and quite possibly the route Bruce would have chosen as he sought out the Comyns, also at Inverlochy. I strode on, emerging on the west side of Glen Nevis with Ben Nevis straight ahead and, to the north, views over the flat plain towards Corpach and the long ridge of Druim Fada. I made my way downhill and followed the road out of Glen Nevis.

In a secluded location on the banks of the River Lochy sits the once mighty and still proud Inverlochy Castle (referred to as Old Inverlochy Castle to differentiate it from the luxury hotel and restaurant nearby). A large square keep supported by four strong circular towers was further protected by the River Lochy, which was diverted to form a surrounding moat. It was built in 1280 by John Comyn Lord of Badenoch (father of John Comyn murdered at Greyfriars Kirk) and is exactly how you would imagine a typical medieval castle would look. In 1307, Bruce attacked the castle as he began his journey up the Great Glen. There was no time for a long siege and one of the guards gave the King and his troops access to the fortress which, once captured, was not destroyed, but kept as a royal strength, to oversee the area.

I crossed the river and headed to the Caledonian Canal to meet my family. Nicola had prepared a hearty meal and afterwards I flaked out on the couch of the in-laws caravan. Meg lay equally comatose in her cosy dog bed. The next day I caught up properly on all the goings on back home and in the light of day, as we went for a game of ten pin bowling, I was told I looked drawn and gaunt and that the dog's eyes were sunken. I needed food, the dog needed water. Used to silence as I was, the everyday noise of family life was also a bit of a shock, whilst the everyday items that we all take for granted like satellite TV, food in the cupboards and a sprung mattress still held a novelty that I knew from experience only lasted a day or two before becoming commonplace once more.

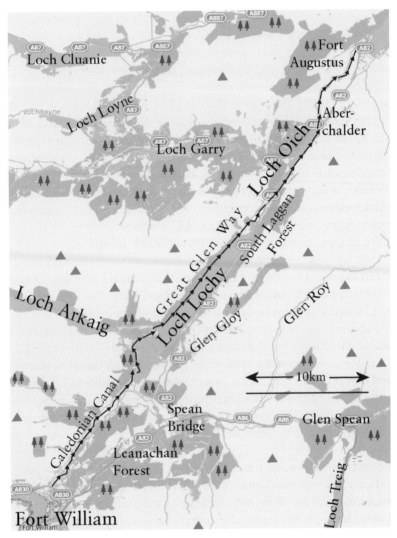

The Great Glen Way.

CHAPTER 5

The Great Glen

THE FOLLOWING MORNING, my brief family reunion over, I took to the road again with fresh supplies and clean clothes. Nicola and the kids had their Easter holidays ahead of them so I would see them at some point before they returned home. My journey resumed at Neptune's Staircase, a picturesque series of eight lock gates on the Caledonian Canal, where boats and barges are lifted from sea level up a height of 20m to begin their journey along the Great Glen. In 1822, it was one of the engineering feats of its day and watching the boats progress remains an absorbing sight.

Hiking one of Scotland's Great Trails, the Great Glen Way, I would be chasing the King of Scots along a geological fault line that separates the Grampian Mountains from the northwest Highlands. Bruce was aiming for Urquhart Castle on the banks of Loch Ness, which was occupied by the forces of another adversary, the Earl of Ross. William, the 3rd earl, controlled a huge swathe of mainland Scotland north of the Great Glen – Ross being one of the seven territories that Celtic Scotland was divided into before the coming of the Normans. As a Sheriff, William also exerted control over islands of the Hebrides including Lewis, Skye, the Uists and Barra. A firm supporter of the Balliols, he was a key enemy with whom Bruce would have to contend to gain control in northern Scotland.

The 118km of the Great Glen Way can be strode, rode, or sailed and, unlike me, a common foot soldier, Bruce probably did a bit of all three as he made his way along an ancient route. I followed the canal towpath uphill, along the side of the lock gates, with Ben Nevis rising into the clouds on the starboard side. This was familiar terrain for me, as I had walked my dogs here during numerous caravan holidays; a narrow tunnel under the canal allowed a circular walk back to the car park at Banavie. From a second underpass, a farm road leads towards

The Great Glen Way. The Caledonain Canal on the left, the River Lochy on the right.

the River Lochy. Parallel to the road, a section of track known as Banquo's walk heads for the remains of Tor Castle. Fifteen hundred years before Fort William became the outdoor capital of the UK, Tor Castle may have been the site of the capital of the Dalriadic Scots, 'Beregonium.'[17]

With the wind at my back, I made good time. I was shunted along to Gairlochy, where the canal joins up with Loch Lochy and a little pepperpot lighthouse directs boats from the loch into the canal, Loch Lochy being the first of three waterways to be navigated as vessels make their way along the Great Glen. The footpath soon found the lochside and continued on a mossy carpet amongst native woodland before heading into a conifer plantation at Fairy Forest, where an enchanting collection of fairies reside, hidden amongst the trees. A short section of road took me past the entrance to Achnacarry Castle, ancestral home of the Camerons of Lochiel. During World War II it was nicknamed Castle Commando with more than 30,000 elite soldiers based there for training in the surrounding mountains. By the lochside were the remains of a model D-Day landing craft where commandos practiced disembarking, as live ammunition was fired overhead. At Clunes Bay I passed some ancient and gigantic Scots pines, which although not old enough to have seen the Bruce, may well have witnessed Bonnie Prince Charlie's passing. After his defeat at Culloden, Charles Edward Stuart hid out in this area before he was led to the security of Cluny's Cage in the mountains of Badenoch. I continued on a forest road which ran the length of Loch Lochy and underneath the Munros of Meall na Teanga and Sron a Choire Ghairbh. Ahead, a couple of speedy walkers kept me focused during this long section, as I tried vigorously to reel them in. Reaching Laggan, where another section of the Caledonian Canal connects Loch Lochy to Loch Oich, I made for the Eagle Barge, which was moored alongside the path. To escape a fierce rainstorm I headed down into the hold – not a dark and claustrophobic storeroom but a roomy, well lit restaurant/cafe, adorned with memorabilia, collections and historical bits and pieces. Here at last, I caught up with the couple whom I had been tailing and, setting the café owners up for life, I had a coffee and a Kit Kat. When the rain abated, I continued along the canalside to Loch Oich, passing the restored platform of Invergarry Station, on the defunct Fort William to Fort Augustus railway. The equivalent of £20 million pounds was spent in 1833 to lay the tracks and build the connecting tunnels, bridges and stations, but the builder's grand vision of eventually linking with Inverness was never realised and the railway closed in the 1940s. Looking for a camping spot, I walked along the shore of Loch Oich on a narrow path before fallen trees forced me up a steep embankment onto the track bed of the old railway. Later, back down by the lochside again, I squeezed my tent into a tight little space, following my general rule not to spend hours looking for the perfect spot. If a site did the job (ie level, dry and private) I just stopped, assembled and ate. On this occasion, I would have been better hanging on. The next morning I found a perfect spot for camping just a kilometre further on at the fabulously named Trailblazer Rest, where there is a flat, grassy pitching area, fire pits and a composting toilet. On the other side of the loch, there was at one time even better accommodation: on Raven Rock are the towering remains of Invergarry Castle, the last Scottish castle in which Bonnie Prince Charlie slept. Ancestral home of the MacDonnells of Glengarry, it has remained a burned-out shell since 1746 when it was torched by the Duke of Cumberland's redcoats. Below Raven Rock, there is partially sunken accommodation: the *Eala Bhan*, a 20m converted herring drifter, wrecked in 2010.

I passed a viaduct with crenelated battlements, a relic of the old railway, and crossed a wide iron bridge where a substantial part of the £20 million could now be recouped in scrap. At Aberchalder, the River Oich leaves the loch and accompanied by the Caledonian Canal it runs into Fort Augustus, where a series of lock gates bring the height of the canal down to the same level as that of Loch Ness. The canal splits the village and crowds were gathered to watch a flotilla of boats, yachts and a British Navy training vessel, HMS *Exploit*, descend. Loch Ness is by far the biggest of the enclosed lochs within the Great Glen; it is deeper than any other Scottish loch and contains more water than all the lakes and rivers of England and Wales combined!

At a picnic bench, I had lunch in the developing rain and then hurried on into the forest that covers the north bank of the loch. A couple of hours later I reached Invermoriston and despite the shelter of the woods I was soaked through. Crossing the River Moriston, I looked over to the old bridge (1813). I mention roads, bridges and canals so often because the later social history of the Highlands is wrapped up in these communications. In the 18th century, following the Jacobite Risings, military roads and bridges were brought to the then untamed Highland terrain by Generals Wade and Caulfield as part of the government's attempts to exert control. A side effect of this was that the most rugged part of Great Britain ended up becoming the best mapped. Thomas Telford continued building infrastructure in the 19th century in an effort to improve Highland communities, decimated by impoverishment and emigration. These roads, bridges and canals are now 200–300 years old. Built to survive Highland weather conditions, surviving the passage of time has been easy.

I took shelter in the porch of the Glen Moriston Arms Hotel whilst waiting for the bar to open, but ten minutes before the taps began to pour, the sun came out, so I set off to walk myself dry. Climbing steeply uphill on a back road, I turned off into the forest once more, where native species were interspersed with conifers. Beside the path,

Welcome shelter in a cave above Loch Ness.

a cave – a rock overhang for a roof and in the interior, a bench built from slabs of stone. This cosy little shelter was the perfect place for an early dinner.

Descending to Allt Sigh, I briefly entertained trying to find accommodation at the youth hostel, but I steeled myself to continue by asking myself the question: 'What are you Gregor? A man or a mouse? This brought back teenage memories of being sick after smoking a celebratory cigar, having completed a hike with friends. One of my pals turned to me and asked the above question in front of the group, to my eternal shame. Suitably chastened by the memory, I carried on purposefully uphill once more and onto a wide ridge above the pines. Walking alone in the grey light at the end of the day as the temperature dropped was often eerie and the senses sharpened expectantly. On this occasion it was especially so. When I plunged back into the pines, the path narrowed, trees touched overhead and mist hung lazily in the gap below.

Even in the midst of thick woods, it was punishingly cold during the night, not helped by the fact I was sleeping in damp clothes to try and dry them out. Not my brightest idea! In the morning, hurrying for a hot pick-me-up, a nasty shock awaited: sipping from my mug, something bumped repeatedly against my top lip. Looking down my nose, I saw a fat black slug floating in my coffee and couldn't help retching. Thank God I hadn't swallowed down the coffee in big gulps.

Paul Theroux once said that travelling is part escapism, part arrival. Escapism: fleeing from routines, expectations and worries. Although happy to be rid of these modern binds for a while, I was also trying to escape the changes of the last 700 years and visualise a 14th-century world. This is comparatively easy in the Scottish Highlands, because so much remains undisturbed by modern man. It is easy to imagine that round the next corner there could be a party of mud splattered knights on horseback, or a wandering friar with news from the south.

Emerging from the trees into bright sunlight, I chased a snorting sheep and its lamb along a very minor and narrow road, passing the wonderfully named hamlets of Grotaig, Balbeg and Ancarraig to reach Upper Lenie – where I hoped to find a path down to Urquhart Castle. On arriving at this little hamlet, there was no sign of the path and according to the map its route went through someone's garden. I approached the house and knocked on the door but got no response, so I went to chap some other doors. Between houses I met Della, who offered to help and put me on the right track alongside Borlum Wood. At nearby Strone, I could see the castle jutting out into the loch far below. Taking a shortcut near a cottage, I yomped across a field, much to the watching owner's bemusement/annoyance (I couldn't tell which). The land veered steeply downhill, as I made a futile charge down upon a legendary stronghold.

Like 250,000 people annually, I sat and watched a short film summarising the history of Urquhart Castle, before it was delightfully revealed. A network of stairs, paths and passages take you round the substantial ruins. In its heyday it was a massive fortification fought over numerous times during the Wars of Independence; heroic tales of defiance abound on both sides. The 13th-century citadel was greatly expanded by the Comyns, demonstrating not only their power and wealth but the strategic importance of the Great Glen. Their castles of Inverlochy and Urquhart were by far the biggest structures in the surrounding landscape. As the Christians built their churches on pagan sites to show that they were the new boys in town, so the Comyns did the same. These dominating fortifications were a massive investment in the area by the Comyn family, who surely thought they were in for the long haul with their 'Shock and Awe' tactics. However, by 1307, the castle was under the control of the Earl William of Ross, who had been on the English side since the defeat of John Balliol in 1296. Unfortunately, there are no details of what methods Bruce used to capture the castle but it must have been a stratagem of some sort as the King had neither the men, nor the time, to afford a traditional siege. By capturing and destroying this fortress, Bruce sent out a strong message to William, right on the southern border of his earldom. Around this time, the Earl of Ross wrote to the King of England saying that he had not enough forces to defend his earldom and that he had received no support from Edward's lieutenant in the north. Furthermore, William's own vassal, Lauchlan MacRuarie of Skye, had risen up against him. The surrounded Earl explained that he had no option but to make a truce with Bruce – obviously on the King's terms because it excluded Inverness Castle which became Bruce's next target.

By mid-afternoon, I was at the adjoining villages of Lewiston and Drumnadrochit, home of Glenurquhart Shinty Team. In Bruce's day, the game of shinty was seen as good warrior training, unlike football and golf which were routinely banned by later Scottish Kings.

Back on the Great Glen Way, I strolled along an avenue of ancient oaks before climbing uphill and taking a last, lingering look back towards Urquhart Bay and its magnificent guardian. I found the signage to be excellent on this route. Up on the hills above Loch Ness, an information board explains that hidden within the surrounding forest are the remains of a Canadian Lumber Camp from the Second World War. The timber chopped, drawn and transported from here was used in the war effort. Leaving the forest temporarily, the path levels off and turns away northwest, crossing the hills and dropping down to Abriachan. I ate and rested briefly at a community woodland area, watching some kids throw a stick for Meg, who obligingly returned it time after time, her collie instinct overcoming her tiredness. Continuing

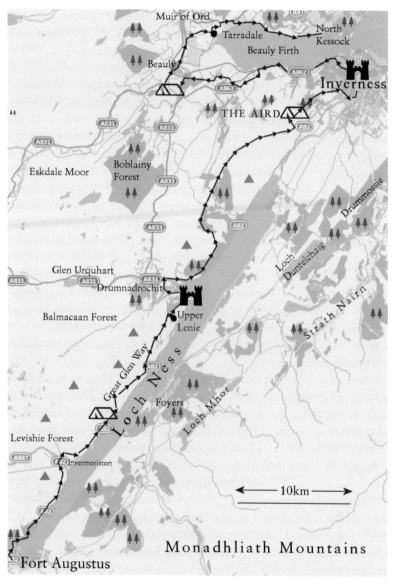

Loch Ness and the Beauly Firth.

on the narrowest of paths between prickly gorse, I ended the day on the outskirts of Inverness in an area known as 'The Aird'. Setting up camp in some woodland, I sat until long after dark, contentedly exhausted, warming my hands on my hobo fire, watching the sparks fly.

Inverness certainly did its best to impress as I entered on a sunny morning. Crossing a golf course and then the Caledonian Canal, I walked past a sports centre, leisure centre, botanic gardens, rugby club and Whin Leisure Park. If this wasn't enough to convince a Great Glen Way'er to relocate, the next part of the walk certainly did. I crossed the River Ness via the endearing Ness Islands – mini woodland parks all connected together by suspension foot bridges. Overlooking the city, lodged on a cliff, sits Inverness Castle – a 19th-century affair, Bonnie Prince Charlie's clansmen having blown up the previous incarnation. The mock sandstone castle crowned with decorative battlements serves as a Sheriff Court and is not open to the public. Bruce laid siege to the 14th-century version, which surrendered when the garrison ran out of water. Thereafter the King completely destroyed it. The castle grounds are the terminus of the Great Glen Way and I had managed the 118km in 3.5 days. While I was enjoying a celebratory bowl of soup in the nearby Castle Tavern, the barman presented me with a certificate for my efforts.

Bruce went on to put more pressure on the Earl of Ross by attacking the town of Nairn and then another fortification at Tarradale on the north shore of the Beauly Firth. Tackling the castle first, I headed out of Inverness following the main road west, along the southern shore of the firth which separates Inverness-shire from the Black Isle.

Although I had been told there was a wide verge alongside the main road, it was a difficult and dangerous journey walking alongside the busy route. Sometimes the verge disappeared as the road was squeezed between the shore and the railway line. At last, halfway to my evening's destination, Beauly, I escaped onto more relaxing back roads at Inchberry House. Apart from one of us spooking a horse and nearly unseating the rider (who is Damian, me or Meg?) the rest of the afternoon was uneventful. I stayed at Lovat Bridge Campsite so that I could get a decent spruce up, as I had a meeting the following day.

An ancient elm tree and Beauly Priory.

A cockerel's cry awoke me at who knows what time o'clock and I eventually succumbed to its insistent demand for action. I was on the road before 8am, crossing the River Beauly at Thomas Telford's Lovat Bridge, entering into the Earldom of Ross. In the centre of the little town of Beauly are the ruins of the 13th-century priory. The Valliscaulian order was sister to that at Ardchattan; headquarters was Burgundy, France, a 40-day trip in medieval times. Making this dangerous journey was not in itself enough, it seems, to escape criticism – one monk who made the journey south was berated for not bringing any salmon. The order believed in poverty, chastity and obedience; only the prior was allowed to have any contact with the outside world and the monks themselves obeyed a vow of silence. Quite possibly Bruce would have demanded food and accommodation from the monks. An ancient elm at the entrance gate may well have waved at the passing of his army.

Soon I was on farm tracks surrounded by fields and made my way to the northwest of Tarradale House. Inverness Wildfowlers Association provided atmosphere with some timely gunfire as I approached an untended grassy mound within a field of barley which denoted the site of Tarradale Castle.

In 1304, the castle was described as one of the strongest in the country.[18] It was captured and destroyed by Bruce's army, but not before the Earl of Ross and his son had withdrawn once more. The King had entered the Earl's territory and destroyed his premier stronghold. William, Earl of Ross, did not commit himself to battle, either because he did not have the forces to take on Bruce's highly mobile army or because he preferred to wait and see if Bruce's ascendancy was going to be something of permanence. If it was, then attempts could be made to switch allegiance.

There are no above-ground remains of the castle. I came, I saw, but I wondered why I'd bothered! This was as far north as Bruce reached in 1307–08 and I traipsed back to the Beauly Firth, following the shore, watching the tide race in over the mud flats. I rested briefly at Milton of Redcastle, under the shadow of a stunning but sadly ruinous and uncared-for 17th-century castle. Keeping an eye on the surviving birdlife, mainly oyster catchers and shelducks, I made my way along the quiet shore-hugging road passing through Charlestown, a neat and tidy little village, closely followed by North Kessock. A little early for my meeting, I sat on the front porch of the local hotel with a coffee and relaxed.

In the company of Ian Jardine, the Managing Director of Scottish National Heritage (SNH), I crossed the Beauly Firth on the Kessock Bridge; a ferry would have operated in Bruce's day. With a companion, I completely forgot my surroundings as we chatted about my journey so far. If I completed my walk then over half of the 1,000 miles would have been on Scotland's Great Trails – 14 of the 26 would have been traipsed to some degree. The marketing of the Great Trails came under the stewardship of SNH and Ian was giving me some moral support. In the past weeks I had walked considerable parts of the Ayr Coastal Path, West Highland Way, Clyde Walkway and Great Glen Way.

Arriving in Inverness I thanked Ian, who, despite a back injury and busy schedule, had taken time out to walk with me. He directed me down Longman Road, past the car dealerships and I crossed the A9 at the Raigmore Interchange, heading for Nairn along the busy A96, the main route to Aberdeen. A footpath continued alongside the road

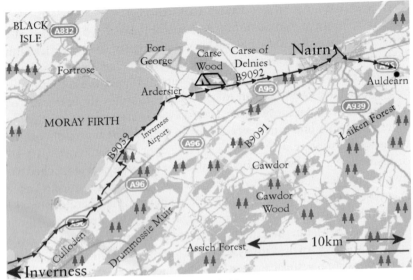

Inverness to Auldearn.

until I reached Milton of Culloden, where it stops suddenly. With the verge narrowing and the cars getting faster, I opted for the safety of the adjoining fields, louping fences as best I could. Not until I was out in front of the farmer's house did the combined weight of the dog, the rucksack and me bring down a fence. That little field happened to contain hens, geese and a duck pond, so I had no option but to stay and try and fix the damage, expecting a shotgun pellet in my rear end at any minute. A short distance later, I turned off the main road at last and onto a back road heading towards Ardersier. Exhausted, I bypassed the village and camped a couple of kilometres further on, hidden in the bosom of Smithstown Wood. Low on water, I had only enough for dinner and I felt extremely guilty the next morning when Meg was so thirsty that she started licking the condensation off the tent.

Next up, Nairn, a popular seaside town on the Moray Firth. King James VI once remarked that the High Street was so long that the people at either end spoke different languages – the fishermen speaking Gaelic at one end, the farmers at the other end speaking Scots. I checked for traces of Robert Bruce at the museum, but there were none although the assistant tried to convince me that he had slept in a house in the High Street. I nearly fell for it, but eventually the penny dropped and I realised she was mixing up Robert Bruce with Robert Burns. A castle *was* located just off the High Street at Castle Lane, but the site has been built over. When Bruce passed through in 1307 he demonstrated his unmolested power and further intimidated the Earl of Ross by burning the town. I walked down to the harbour where the whistling wind was blowing stoutly and the masts on the boats were rattling madly; people leaving the sheltered, narrow streets of Fishertown were almost blown off their feet when they reached the promenade. I sat and surveyed the scene from the comfort of a beach shelter, where the luxury of milk made my porridge and coffee a whole lot more palatable.

Situated in the middle of the nearby village of Auldearn, there is a large motte, topped by a 17th-century dovecote. In September 1308, the year following his burning of the town, Bruce returned here and within a wooden castle which stood on the earthen mound, he received the formal submission of the Earl of Ross. The reduction of the fortresses in the Great Glen; the burning of Nairn; Bruce's advance into Ross; the destruction of Tarradale Castle; the lack of support from England; the defeating of the MacDougalls; the ejection of the Comyns (more on this next); and the uprising of the Earls' own vassals, conspired to give him no option but to submit to the Bruce. Putting aside personal enmity, the King showed political nous in his dealings with this nobleman, who had taken his Queen and daughter from sanctuary and sent them to England to face the wrath of Edward I. There they would yet remain for another six years. The terms offered to the Earl to switch allegiance were generous – he kept all his lands, and in fact was granted more. William of Ross became a determined and loyal supporter, as did his son Hugh, who in later years was given further patronage as well as being allowed to marry Bruce's sister, Matilda. The King, having failed to make any permanent headway in the southwest, had come north and was now conquering Scotland in reverse.

CHAPTER 6

The Garioch, Buchan and Aberdeen

AFTER BURNING NAIRN, Bruce continued his conquest of Moray by attacking Elgin and its lofty castle. The King of Scots was heading for a showdown with the major power in the northeast, his bitter rivals the Comyns.

Once more, I headed for the peace and quiet of back roads and soon reached the Culbin Forest, which runs alongside the Moray Firth coastline and offers shelter from the sea breeze. The land here was farmed until 1694, when a huge storm deposited enough sand to cover the whole area, submerging the buildings and destituting the people. For the next two hundred years the area was left as shifting sand dunes, Scotland's Sahara, before the Forestry Commission managed to stabilise the ground and plant its forests.[19]

At the Royal Burgh of Forres, I halted at the Victoria Hotel for a drink and bowl of soup, while I recharged my phone. Later, as I strolled along a High Street dominated by an imposing tolbooth, I noticed a healthy lack of 'To Let' signs. At the edge of town is Sueno's Stone, a magnificent 6m tall standing stone, dating to the 9th or 10th century. Carved upon one side is a ring-headed cross; the other side depicts a battle scene displayed in four panels. Who exactly is fighting has not been established, partly because in the early days of the Kingdom of Scotland, Moray was the scene of much conflict. Thus, it may be the Scots defeating the Picts, or the Scots and Picts together defeating the Vikings, or it may even be the men of Moray defeating and decapitating King Dubh in 966AD. It survived, probably, because it was buried in the ground during some of Scotland's most turbulent times and was not rediscovered until the 18th century. Now it is protected, not so much from the people but from the atmosphere, in a large glass case.

Later that evening, trying to find a private place to camp not too far from the road, I fought a battle to gain entry to a patch of scrub, trying

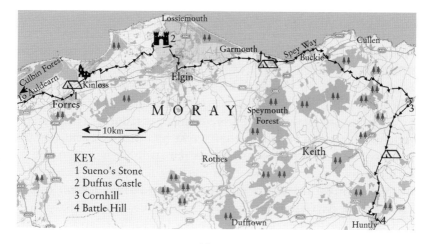

Moray.

to work my way around gorse and spruce. At the first flat, dry patch, I set about clearing a space. Once in the tent, Meg seemed to be on edge – sitting up with ears pricked listening intently, barking intermittently – giving our position away to anyone interested. I imagined the army from nearby Kinloss, out on a night exercise, creeping by. The final disturbance was either fireworks or a gun party, I was too tired to look, before silence reigned, broken only by the welcome, haunting call of the curlews in nearby Findhorn Bay. In the morning, I awoke to a wonderful vista: a huge area of mudflats connected to the sea only by a narrow inlet and framed by clear blue sky streaked with just an occasional, harmless, cirrus cloud. Following the edge of the bay, I came to Kinloss and the last ruins of a great religious house. For 400 years the abbey was a dominant, prosperous force in the area until the Reformation in 1560. The Cistercian monks lived an austere life, but developed an economy based on the exploitation of land and the abbey became a wealthy institution. The church estates were sold in the post-Reformation land grab and the church buildings denuded in 1650 when the stone was sold to Oliver Cromwell, who was building a citadel in Inverness.

The Reformation can be decried for the damage that was done

to Scotland's religious houses and anything else seen to be remotely idolatrous. However, leaving aside religious beliefs, the Reformation laid the foundations for an education system that would benefit the majority of the population, a vital element in the makeup of the many Scots who went on to make their way in the world so remarkably when the opportunities came in the 18th and 19th centuries.

King Edward I stayed at Kinloss Abbey in 1303, during a triumphant progress through Scotland – in two weeks his army ate a whole year's worth of food. Bruce's visit is not remembered, but he was trying to establish his authority rather than enjoying the fruits of victory. He made a grant to the abbey in 1312 of the valuable salmon fishing rights for the River Findhorn.[20]

Carrying on through the village, I passed by Kinloss Barracks, home to 1,000 personnel from 39 Engineer Regiment, better known in its previous guise as RAF Kinloss (1939–2012). I headed towards Duffus Castle. The luxurious houses under construction in secluded spots along the way gave me a few pangs of envy as I passed by, carrying my home on my back – snail-like, also, in speed. My jealousy was only skin deep: I knew that my walk was, at least in part, a rejection of materialism, an attempt to prove that I could prosper without everyday conveniences. In the 19th century, writer and philosopher Henry David Thoreau railed against an increasingly materialistic society and went to the woods to live in a tiny cabin, the modern conveniences he was rejecting were plastered walls, a large cellar, a lock on the door and venetian blinds – try passing these features off as luxuries to the typical house buyer today and see what you get. Luxury is of course relative to our expectations but I wasn't finding it any harder to live without my 21st-century equivalents. I was crying out for a simpler life, a back to basics approach; I believed I was proving what Thoreau said – that elevation was to be found in a simple life. It struck me that my simple life required me to make an effort for shelter, food and travel, effort which gave me purpose, fulfilling a man who sometimes found that sense of purpose wanting.

Duffus Castle, a large stone tower built atop an old motte, was the home of Sir Reginald Cheyne, Warden of Moray. Robert Bruce attacked and destroyed the newly built castle in 1308 and although the stonework has been marked by a great fire, no one has said this was the fire of Bruce's men. The outstanding feature of the castle is its partial collapse. A complete corner has broken off and fallen down the unstable motte, where it sits, tilted but secure. Families picnicking on the bailey were exploring the tower and the strange tilted passageway of the giant detached fragment. In sweltering temperatures, I had my own lonely picnic before charging on towards Elgin. Taking a shortcut alongside an overgrown drainage ditch that crossed one of the surrounding fields, I disturbed the sheltering wildlife, including a couple of deer who ran off across the tilled soil, sparking up a cloud of dust like galloping camels in a desert.

It was only a short distance to Elgin, which Bruce captured at the third attempt. The castle itself stood on Lady's Hill in the centre of town and only a few fragments remain. The hilltop is dominated by an extraordinarily large column dedicated to the 5th Duke of Gordon – without denigrating his achievements, others have done a lot more and been venerated a lot less. Elgin was a Royal Burgh in Bruce's time and its mighty 13th-century cathedral was known as the Lantern of the North. This edifice was the seat of the Bishop of Moray. David de Moray was a stalwart for Scottish Independence; in 1303, when just about every other prominent Scot had submitted to Edward I,

Duffus Castle, built on an unstable motte.

Elgin Castle once stood atop Ladyhill.

he remained resolute. David preached to his flock that resisting the English was equivalent to fighting a crusade against the Saracens in the Holy Land. Fleeing to Orkney in 1306 after Bruce's defeat at Methven, he returned to Moray at the same time as Bruce, landed in Ayrshire and did such a good job whipping up support for Bruce's cause that a Scots lord on the English side wrote that Bruce need only come north and the country would rise for him. Bruce duly obliged, and on the back of success in the north was his kingship built.

Continuing east, I stopped and ate within a neglected stone circle at Innesmill, spending a beautiful evening at a monument that was ancient even in Bruce's day. Even the semolina thickened. Perfect! The River Spey is a formidable barrier to east–west progress in Morayshire. Garmouth lies on the west bank, one kilometre from the river mouth. The age of the village is betrayed by its narrow, winding lanes. In 1650, Charles II landed here to reclaim the throne of his decapitated father. I crossed the Spey on a 300m railway viaduct built in 1886 to span the three wide flows of the river and able to sustain a load of 354 tonnes. Even with a fully laden rucksack I wasn't touching this weight so I bounced merrily across.

Camping near the iron behemoth, I arose early, making for Spey Bay. It was a serene, quiet morning and the sea was calm as I approached the little community, which includes a wildlife centre, a

Bruce holding aloft a charter, outside Marishcal College, Aberdeen.

Setting off from Dalrigh, just south of
Tyndrum in the Trossachs.

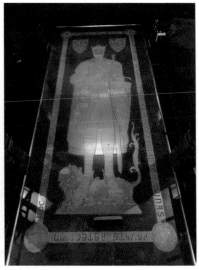

The tomb of Robert the Bruce in
Dunfermline Abbey.

Loch Neldricken hidden in the midst of the Galloway Hills.

Fragmentary remains of Roxburgh Castle.

With just one companion Bruce was pursued down the Nick of the Dungeon by a force of Highlanders led by John MacDougall.

The path to Urquhart Castle, which was besieged and captured by Bruce.

A stunning view of Loch Leven and the Pap of Glencoe from the West Highland Way.

Inverurie was Bruce's base during his critical campaign against the Comyns.

Strolling past Holyrood Abbey.

Sandstone church at Old Cambus.

Dryburgh Abbey, burned by Edward II's army in 1322.

Minchmoor Bothy, a piece of Americana in the Scottish Borders.

An effigy of King Robert the Bruce at St Conan's Kirk, Loch Awe.

The Ewing clan at Bannockburn and Meg, ready for another adventure.

golf course, a former hotel and a huge ice house (built in the early 19th century for storing salmon). It was early, nobody was stirring and I was enveloped by the peacefulness of the place, which seemed to be gradually absorbed within me. I thought of the past, of my grandmother's family, Gordons who hailed from this area; of family members who had enjoyed holidays here. However, thinking of the departed started to become a bit overwhelming, reminding me of my own mortality and so I said goodbye to the ancestors and determined from here on to focus on the future. I was virtually halfway through the walk, in good health and had nothing to complain about.

I was now almost at the northern terminus of the Speyside Way and lost sight of the sea as the markers took me inland through a suffocating pine wood before I emerged onto fields, along which ran the trackbed of a disused railway line. Portgordon, now a quiet little village, was in the 19th century the area's biggest port with the harbour capable of holding 350 ships. Just past the village there was a large colony of seals – both grey and common seals mix here and there were dozens sunning themselves on the rocks. A fella pulled up on his moped to watch this fine natural spectacle and we got chatting. Having lost his job, he had sold his car and bought two motor bikes: a moped and high powered growler. Still getting to grips with the former he was fulfilling his desire to explore the country. As Jim sped

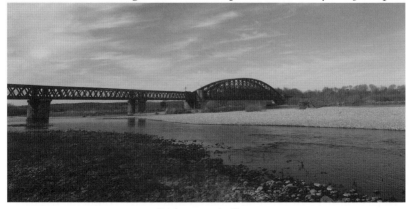

Bridge over the Spey.

off, so to speak, I got talking to Allan who was out walking his pair of brown border collies. He hadn't seen anyone else with a brown border collie in the area and took a shine to Meg. He didn't have any Bruce stories to relate, but told me that during World War II, three German spies were dropped off by a flying boat and made their way in a dinghy, unnoticed, to the shore at Port Gordon. Two of them, a female and male, aroused suspicion at the railway station and were apprehended. The third spy made it to Edinburgh before he too was arrested. Incredibly, their initial plan had been to cycle to London, but the bicycles were lost overboard whilst coming to shore. The two men stood trial and were executed. The female, Vera Erikson, never stood trial and after the war; she was either sent back to Germany or, more intriguingly, lived out her life in southern England. Conspiracy theories abound.[21]

At Buckie, a large fishing town, I said goodbye to the sea for a while and headed inland. Bruce had been intending to continue along the coast to attack Banff Castle, but took ill and his army retreated to Cornhill. I climbed through the Hilton Wood between the Hill of Maud and the Bin of Cullen and for the rest of the afternoon I negotiated unclassified and undulating country roads.

In April 1308, the sheriff of Banff, Duncan of Frendraught, wrote to Edward II. The letter has survived and provides much of the detail we have of Bruce's movements in 1307–08. Bruce stayed at Corncarn Manor for two nights. The mighty Comyn family made a move: the Earl of Buchan with other leading Comyn supporters brought an army to face Bruce, who responded by burning the manor, along with all the grain and some of King Edward's carts, before retreating to Huntly.

I had forgotten to bring notes on Corncarn Manor with me on the walk but I knew it was located in Cornhill and I had it in my mind that I was looking for a ruin. I headed along a track, towards Old Cornhill, which seemed a sensible place to look. There, I spoke to the farmer of 20 years and asked if there were any ancient ruins in the vicinity; he knew of none. Giving up far too easily, I asked him about the track which continued through his property and skirted round the rise called Corn Hill. He said that although it was the old route south, no one had ever used the track during the time he had farmed the land and that it would be near impossible going. It was. I soon gave up on that plan, as the track was overgrown with gorse. Instead, I took to the fields on the slopes of the rise called Corn Hill. I missed the target here, I should have visited the Castle of Park, to the south of Cornhill, which originated in 1292 and is now a private home. Afterwards, from what I saw of Bruce's other campsites, I think the army would have camped at the top of Corn Hill, to the southwest of the castle and which I had skirted around.

From Ordiquhill I continued south towards Huntly, with little choice but to follow the road. Breaking out from the terrain was steeply pointing Knock Hill (where two guys towing a Ford Cosworth on a trailer turned up looking for the racetrack – Knockhill racetrack is near Dunfermline a mere 150-mile drive to the south). As I neared Knockdhu Distillery, a car drove past, turned around and came back towards me; it stopped and a man in slippers jumped out and stuffed a ten pound note into my hand. I was dumbfounded and tried to refuse politely but he wouldn't take no for an answer and insisted that I take the money. He said he had read about my walk in the paper and had just seen me go past his front window. We continued talking and he explained further that he thought I was ex forces. Well, an ex-Jacobite maybe! I described my intended journey and explained that previously I had followed Bonnie Prince Charlie. He said he was really interested in history and that I was to buy some rations. Feeling decidedly guilty, I kept the cash and I promised to send him a copy of my book when I got home.

The next day was Easter Sunday and the roads were respectfully quiet. Even so, I couldn't say the walking was fun. It just had to be endured. At least the weather was nice and hot. After crossing the River Deveron, I followed a bankside path, passing a Nordic ski course on my way towards the substantial remains of Huntly Castle, where a dominating frontage gives illustrative evidence of the wealth once enjoyed by the chiefs of Clan Gordon. Mary of Guise, James v's widow and mother of Mary Queen of Scots, was lavishly entertained here at the grand home of the 4th Earl of Huntly, the 'cock o' the north'. One

Castle Huntly, demonstrative of the Gordon Clan at the height of their powers.

of her courtiers, perhaps jealously, advised her to 'clip his wings', such was his power and influence. In 1562, her daughter's royal army duly did that at the Battle of Corrichie. It was, however, the abandoned motte overlooking the river that interested me. Now just a grassy knoll, this was the site of a 12th-century timber castle built by Duncan, Earl of Fife. Bruce was at the castle, recovering from a debilitating illness. He had possibly lain here before, but more probably after, the skirmish, which had taken place just outside the town of Huntly. Leaving the castle grounds, following an avenue designed to impress brought me right into the little town of Huntly, which is centred on an attractive square. I bought some delicious smelling 'butteries', a high energy, savoury roll that is a local speciality and headed to Battle Hill. The origin of how the hill got its name is disputed but it would seem to be the obvious place for the Comyn army to have made its base as they faced off Bruce's army encamped on another hill further to the east, Robin's Height. I followed a path north, which took me over the hill and then I cut east to try and walk around the battlefield. I called in at a farm on the way but was unable to glean any new information. After walking in a big circle on farm roads and tracks, I came to Slioch

Farm. Gordon the farmer there, was really helpful and interested in the skirmish which had taken place on his land. Together we crossed fields of barley to reach the top of Robin's Height, which is crowned with a small stand of trees. This was the site of Bruce's encampment; the views around are excellent and the hill isolated enough to give plenty warning of approaching enemies.

A local rhyme explains the lie of the land. 'Ba' Hill, Battle Hill, Clashmach and the Bin, they a' form a circle and Huntly lies within.' We looked over to the site of the skirmish – the dip between our stance and Battle Hill – and Gordon explained that the ground at the bottom was marshy, further enhancing the defensive qualities of Bruce's campsite.

On Christmas Day 1307, Comyn and his allies approached Bruce's army but could not see its strength. The King's forces were probably hidden in the trees. An archery battle took place, with Comyn's forces on the lower ground no doubt coming off worse. The stand-off continued for a few days with ongoing skirmishing. Finally, the armies squared up and the nerve of the Comyn leadership failed when Bruce's forces, and possibly a partially recovered King, revealed themselves. The two parties then agreed a truce. Bruce remained unwell and stayed in the area for a further week before heading southeast to Inverurie. He was so ill that he was carried on a litter. The fact that all this took place in December certainly could not have helped Bruce's condition.

Looking over the ground where the skirmish at Slioch took place. Bruce's troops were stationed on the distant hilltop, now crowned by a stand of trees.

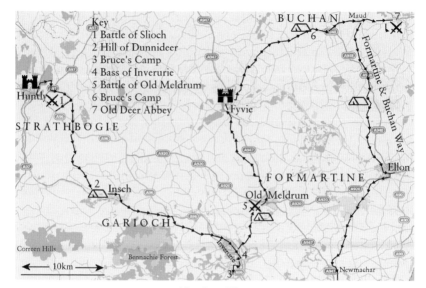

Huntly to Ellon.

The shelter of Huntly Castle must have offered some comfort and an escape from the cold.

Having experienced a section of the A96 as I left Inverness, I had no wish to go anywhere near it again as I followed Bruce to Inverurie. Once more I took quiet, winding back roads, feeling high-spirited as I sang my oddball collection of songs. In past walks I have enjoyed a sing-song to keep up the spirits but have often been frustrated by not knowing the complete lyrics to any songs. Repeating the choruses soon got boring. This time I had brought the words with me, so I walked along, reading from my song sheet and singing heartily, if not tunefully.

Thirteen quick kilometres later and I was at the foot of a hill on which stood Dunnydeer Tower. I walked halfway up and camped in the shelter of some trees. Although I was closer to the path than I would have liked, it was dusk and I was tired, past caring about what people might think. I intended to be away early.

The dog walkers were up before me and as I packed up the tent Meg got mugged. A woman passed with three large dogs and one of

Bennachie, 'the sphynx of the Garioch'.

the mutts distracted my companion with a bit of bum sniffing, whilst the other two buried their noses into her rucksack, which I had left lying unzipped. Without screaming blue murder at her dogs, which I feel should have been her first reaction, she calmly asked me, 'Is there food in that bag?' Turning round, I raced to retrieve the rucksack, shooing the thieving canines away. Food was strictly rationed and Meg worked her paws off to carry her rucksack each day. I was damned if I was going to let them get one more morsel.

I walked up to the summit of this isolated hill and surveyed the remains of 13th-century Dunnydeer Tower. It didn't take me long – there was a gable end and a window! I descended. Gordon from Slioch Farm told me he thought Robert the Bruce had been here and it looked a likely place to have stopped on the way to Inverurie.

From Insch, I took the B9002 and headed east on flat terrain in an area called the Garioch (pronounced Geerie); Bruce had lands here, gained through his first marriage – a place where he could expect to raise an army and where he could hope to establish a secure base from which to direct operations in the northeast. As I walked towards Inverurie, lying below the southern sky was the ridge of Bennachie, an outlier of the Grampian Mountains. The most easterly top is Mither Tap, the head of what W Douglas Simpson brilliantly calls 'the sphinx of the Garioch'.[22]

Forced into the briefest of encounters with the A96, at the first opportunity I turned south and climbed up towards the Maiden Stone, which is situated at the edge of a minor road. This 9th-century Pictish stone is in excellent condition. Carved in relief and highlighted by the bright sunshine are four panels containing Pictish symbols: a mirror and comb; a notched tuning fork, interlaced with a z-rod; an unidentified beast; and on the more weathered top panel, animals and what might have been a centaur. Like many others, I find these symbols fascinating and I struck up a conversation with a couple from Aberdeen about possible meanings of the images. When we got round to Robert the Bruce, the young lady told me her dad was in a local band, Hedgehog Pie, which had just recorded a song about him.

Reaching Inverurie, which was made a Royal Burgh by Robert the Bruce, I purchased camping gas at the outdoor shop and with

The Maiden Stone in glorious sunshine.

Meg breaking the ice, the staff were good enough to charge my mobile phone for me. I just had to make sure I did my touring and returned before closing time. It was mid-afternoon as I rushed off southwards through the town and crossed the mighty River Don. Bruce's camp was, as usual, located in a strong defensive site: a low hill, partially looped-around by the river. Just off the main road, I put my rucksack down and started tearing up old ferns in an effort to conceal it. In my haste, I tore a lump out of my hand; the dried out ferns were razor sharp and I rushed away sucking up the blood from my throbbing palm. I approached a house to ask permission to walk through the farm buildings and get up onto the hill. Lifting my hand to ring the bell, I saw it was covered in blood. Catching the drips with my other hand, I sucked profusely. As the door opened, I shoved my hands behind my back and rubbed my bloody whiskers with my sleeve. If the unsuspecting lady had peeked out the window before coming to the door, she would never have answered it. Instead, she would have called the police, claiming that a blooded, breathless maniac was at her door. Passing through the farm, I climbed upwards through an

The Bass of Inverurie.

unkept field of long grass, onto a hilltop ringed with birch trees; the flat summit area was covered in tussocks of grass and crisscrossed with old, drystane dykes. Another fantastic defensive site – great views all around and the northern and eastern approaches guarded by the River Don.

I jogged off the hill, collected my rucksack, applied a large dog plaster to my hand and headed back into town, to a cemetery located on low ground enclosed by the rivers Don and Urie. Amongst the headstones were two large grassy mounds, the motte and bailey of Inverurie Bass. The higher of the two mounds was particularly steep-sided and accessed by a winding path; atop this mound would have been a wooden palisade and within that a timber castle. The lower mound would have been the courtyard and the two hillocks were at one time connected by a drawbridge. Bruce made Inverurie Castle his hospital and his base for directing operations against his enemies, chief of whom were the Comyns, the most powerful family in Scotland and whose chief landholding, the Earldom of Buchan, was only a few miles away. When Bruce arrived here in January 1308 he was still at war with the Earl of Ross as well as the English-appointed Warden of Moray, Reginald Cheyne. Basing himself here, gathering recruits and receiving fealty from local men, the King used his army to strike fast, not only surprising his enemies, but preventing them from linking up. Had the combined forces of the Earl of Ross, Reginald Cheyne and the Comyns got together, then undoubtedly Bruce would have been defeated. As it was, Bruce was able to attack towns and castles of his choosing, picking them off one by one. Whenever danger threatened his base, he could withdraw across the Don to the hilltop camp.

I made it back to the outdoor store before closing time, collected my phone and headed to Lidl for supplies. Going shopping when you're hungry is never the best idea, particularly when you have to carry everything. Anyway, when I'd finished my shopping I couldn't fit all the supplies into my rucksack. I sat outside the door, trying to avoid the pitying looks as I ravenously devoured all that I couldn't carry, then stuffed the rest into Meg's pack. I crossed the River Urie and headed towards the Hill of Barra on the road to Old Meldrum. On the south side of the hill the landowner, Ian, gave me a grass field all to myself for the evening. Apart from the noisy crows, it was bliss.

From the summit of the Hill of Barra I wanted to survey the site of the variously named Battle of Barra/Inverurie/Old Meldrum, the confusion in the name reflecting the fact the battle took place over a wide area. The path cut uphill towards fields of livestock. Beside a stile, in a field full of sheep, a ewe was licking clean its newborn lamb. The adjoining field held cattle, which Meg and I always seemed to unsettle, so I went back the way I had come.

In March 1308, Bruce's forces were attacked at Inverurie by Sir David de Brechin leading an advance guard of the Earl of Buchan's army. Bruce's forces retreated across the Dee and Buchan's main force were too far behind to follow up the attack. The King, who was sick at the time, was put on his horse and supported thereafter. Confounding the enemy, Bruce's forces launched a vigorous counter-attack against Buchan's army, which lined up in front of Old Meldrum. The aggressive assault and the sight of the mounted King demoralised Buchan's levies. They fled and the battle turned into a rout. Bruce's line of advance is the route of the road between Inverurie and Old Meldrum. This was dangerously busy, so I checked with a farmer that he wouldn't mind if Meg and I charged along the edges of his fields. Trying to imagine the scene, there I was suddenly in the vanguard of Bruce's army.

'The King is well,' they tell us. Our troop of local guys who I know right well, are fighting beside our sons, brothers and fathers. We'll protect one another. Bruce has put a group of captains amongst us, so-called veterans who cajole us forward and stiffen our resolve with great promises and awful threats. Fulfilling our feudal duty to our lord, who also happens to be our bloody King. Ach, what difference will this King make? If we survive the day, the best we can hope for is a bit a peace for a while. At least if we do win, there'll be no more English taxes and maybe less use of the noose. In the distance, a heaving throng of men, lined up against us, waving scythes and spears. Bampots from Buchan! Our pace increases, no relenting, no speeches before battle. Onwards we charge with breathless, rasping cries of encouragement still coming from that bloody annoying Sassenach.

Falling into a drainage ditch brought me back to reality and I left the fields to join a proper path that led into Old Meldrum. Plonked beside a roundabout on the edge of town was Bruce's stone – moved from the Hill of Barra where he reputedly sat and watched the battle – although this doesn't quite match written accounts that say the sight of the mounted King demoralised his enemies. I headed through the town quickly, keeping my head down in the wet conditions. Bruce's forces chased the routers all the way to Fyvie Castle, 10km to the north, and I thought I'd better do the same. After half an hour I escaped the main road and followed farm tracks which ran parallel to the main route north.

In 1308, Fyvie was a royal castle held by lieutenants of the English King. Whether it fell to Bruce's forces at the time of the rout is not known, but it had certainly fallen within a few months. Nowadays it is a magnificent castle from the outside and a treasure trove on the inside.

Fyvie Castle. Magnificent outside and a treasure trove within.

I was given a whirlwind guided tour, requesting to visit the oldest bits of the fortress – the charter-room, the old guardroom of the gatehouse, the drawing room, the great hall – passing portraits by Raeburn and a collection of arms on the walls of the spiral staircase. The highlight of my visit was seeing an ancient iron portcullis, wrought so intricately that we don't know how they did it.

There was one final reckoning to be had with the Earl of Buchan's forces. This took place on a hillside near the village of Old Deer, 24km to the northeast, in the heart of the earldom; thus to Aikey Brae I made my way. The late afternoon and early evening were spent on farm roads, but my head was elsewhere as I rehearsed answers to possible questions that might come up in a feature that STV North were doing on Bruce, Meg and me, the following day. Bruce's Hill, 2km west of New Deer Village, is thought to be the site of Edward Bruce's campsite prior to marching upon the Comyns at Aikey Brae (the King himself was still weakened by illness at this time). The low rise, hardly distinct from the surrounding area, was under crop as I approached, so I went to the nearest farmhouse to ask for permission to camp in the vicinity. Despite the lateness of my arrival, Barbara and Alastair listened to my story and invited me in for a cup of tea. Meg mooched around, garnering sympathy, playing the part of a half-starved, over-exercised dog impeccably. For me, sitting in the warm farmhouse kitchen, chatting over a hot drink, inhaling the smells of fresh baking was delightful. With muscles and senses relaxed, waves of tiredness soon started to wash over me and I thanked my hosts and headed outside into the chilly blackness.

I set off the next morning in thick fog, my hosts kindly having let me use their shower and given me breakfast. My friend Gary, who had kept me going in the past with positive texts sent me a beauty: 'Sunshine is delicious, rain is refreshing, wind braces us up, snow is exhilarating ; there is no such thing as bad weather, only different kinds of good weather.' Fog however was downright dangerous.

As I reached the village of New Deer, my bladder started crying out. (During the walk my bladder acted very strangely – one minute I was fine, the next minute my waters were hammering on the door to get out!) I searched round for facilities and found the Mustard Seed Café. Afterwards, feeling high from the sense of relief, I stayed for a cup of coffee and an empire biscuit and chatted away to a local family.

On the road, the fog had lifted sufficiently for me to be noticed by a

Aikey Brae stone circle. A last stand was made by the Comyns on the southern slopes of this hill.

passing motorist. The car stopped and the fella inside asked me how I was getting on. He said he had enjoyed my book and asked me where I was going this time.

'How did you know it was me?' I asked.

'I didn't recognise you, I recognised the dug.'

Bah, I thought. I do all the writing and the dog gets all the glory.

At the village of Maud, I joined the Formartine and Buchan Way, a long-distance footpath following the railway bed of the dismantled Formartine and Buchan Railway. It was a relief to be walking off-road again. Apart from a short stretch of the Spey Way I had been walking on roads for the past eight days.

Deer Abbey, just outside the village of Old Deer, in the heart of Buchan, was a Cistercian monastery established by the Comyn Family. It was ravaged by Bruce's forces in 1308 and later received compensation for damages sustained. Further decimated many times since, without compensation, the crestfallen remains still retain an air of dignity in a peaceful rural setting by the River Ugie. I met with Ann from STV and she exclaimed, 'You're just how I hoped you would look.' Having been on the go for five weeks, my face had gone brown, my hair had gone white, my beard was multi-coloured and I was thin as a rake. Swap the fleece jacket and stretchy trousers for a ragged shirt and shorts and 'Tonight, Matthew, I will be Robinson Crusoe'. After filming Meg and I strutting our stuff, Ann interviewed me about Bruce's campaign, my own motivations and the contents of Meg's curious rucksack. I felt I knew my subject well, I was living it after all, so that gave me confidence and I didn't stutter or trip over my words too often. The preparation the previous evening definitely helped and the filming was wrapped up in one take. Ann seemed quite pleased and expected the feature would be on the news in the next few days.

Just a short distance away was Parkhouse Hill on the summit of which was Aikey Brae stone circle. As I was following an avenue of gorse uphill, an Alsatian came tearing downhill, followed by a yelling man. The dog had a go at Meg before the puffing owner caught up. Unhappy with the conduct of his canine, I was standoffish at first, but the man seemed oblivious and persisted in talking. When I defrosted,

David explained that he had been responsible for convincing Cambridge University to provide the local history society with digitised images of the 10th-century Book of Deer, an illuminated manuscript, initially kept at a nearby monastery, which found its way to the south of England and then on to the famous institution. The book's fame stems from the fact it contains the oldest known writing in Scots Gaelic.

The hilltop has a large stand of trees and within a clearing at the centre lie the remains of an incumbent stone circle. Approximately 5,000 years old, the incumbent (turned on its side) stone weighs over 20 tons and the other stones vary in height order, getting smaller the further they are from the main stone. Our ancestors were using this site to observe the moon.

This seemed like another good defensive hill position. However, the little information we have is that Bruce's forces met with Comyn's forces on a lower slope called Aikey Brae, where for hundreds of years an annual fair was held. Cattle, horses and general goods were traded here before the funfair became the main attraction in the 20th century. The market was said to have been established in memory of the Bruce's final victory over the Comyns.[23] I went for a look to Aikey Brae itself – just above off the roadside, it was an open meadow with a shallow slope. This didn't seem to me to be a good position for the Comyns to make a last stand: the slope was north-facing and Bruce's troops would be approaching from the west. The hilltop where the stones are situated would have been much better. This site seemed more like a rallying spot for the Earl of Buchan's army or even a hiding place; particularly as aikey may refer to the old Scots word for oak – aik. Much would depend on the choice of routes that an army could travel in the 14th century and if the Comyns' position couldn't be easily outflanked then it may have been reasonable enough. Maybe the Comyns even attempted to ambush Bruce's invading army here. On balance though, I think it was more of a slaughter than a chivalrous battle. A set battle would have been recorded in some of the sources, a slaughter less likely in the pro-Bruce written sources. After this conflict, which resulted in the overthrow of the earl, the Herschip of Buchan began. The main seat of the Comyns, Rattray Castle was destroyed as were the castles of Kinedar, Slains, Dundarg, Cairnbulg, Kelly and possibly others, including Inverallochy. Lands were laid waste, crops and livestock destroyed, homes burned and people killed or dispersed. A cruel destruction of an affluent landscape and an innocent people, upon whose shoulders much of the Comyn powerbase had been built. More smoke belched from the fires started by the King of Scots than ever rose from the flames of Norse attacks, from which the line of castles along the coast had been built to protect.

The Comyns, it must be said, never deserved this fate, having been the stoutest of resistors to Edward I of England. The head of their family had taken the mantle of guardianship and did his utmost to resist English domination. Even when the majority of Scots had capitulated by 1304, John Comyn negotiated not unfavourable terms for his countrymen before submitting to Edward I. Only Bruce's murder of John pushed the Comyns into the bosom of the Edward I and his son. On Bruce's part, the destruction of the Comyns was the platform on which he built the recovery of the Kingdom of Scotland. Eradicating competing factions and unifying the country was Bruce's objective. Only then could he hope to turn and face the immeasurably bigger threat of the King of England.

I walked back to Maud and boarded the Formartine and Buchan Way southwards, the straight and narrow path ploughing its way through rolling farmland. An evening and a morning's walking brought me to the town of Ellon. In Bruce's time Ellon was the capital settlement of Buchanxx where the earl would hold court. The town had developed as a fording place of the River Ythan, over which it was split. Its prominence ensured it was torched by Bruce's forces, so nothing remains from the period. The Herschip of Buchan was lamented for 50 years but it took even longer for Ellon to regain its former prominence. The Earl of Buchan fled to England, the power of the Comyns in the north utterly broken.

Leaving Buchan, I followed the King's forces south as they headed for Aberdeen in an attempt to capture an important trading port from which trading relations could be established. I followed the planes and helicopters towards Dyce, a city suburb, where I camped once again on

Brig o' Balgownie one of the oldest bridges in In Scotland.

a farmer's field. The long distance footpath finished at Dyce but I broke off just before that and headed down to the River Don at Riverside Park, intending to follow it all the way into the city proper. Aberdeen is built between the Rivers Don and Dee, which along with the River Ythan provide the only break in the sandy coastline. Not believing the advice I was given by a couple of local dog walkers, I stuck with the river – and as warned, came to a section that was closed, forcing me to retrace my steps, all the while cursing my blockheadedness. In the end, I chose to follow National Cycle Route 1 into the city and this turned out to be not a bad alternative: swiftly I left the deafening dual carriageway and found myself following quieter back roads into the city. At Seaton Park, a tranquil, green oasis within the city, I headed down to the river once more and soon reached the Brig' o' Balgownie, which spans the Don close to its mouth. This large bridge, one of the oldest in Scotland, has a single 12m span and when viewed from above is shaped like a shepherds crook. It was built on the instructions and at the expense of Robert the Bruce.

Within twin-spired St Machar's Cathedral was a welcome surprise. I nipped in to use the toilet. Not wanting to be too obvious, I was having a wee cross-legged wander when I found, hanging on the wall, a beautifully carved oak triptych dedicated to John Barbour, Archdeacon of Aberdeen, whose *The Bruce* is the earliest major work of Scottish literature as well as a major source of information on Robert the Bruce's life.

I headed south along the cobbled streets of Aberdeen University and had lunch under the cloisters, watching the students come and go. For a long time, Aberdeen had two universities, the same number as in all of England. In the city centre, in front of Marischal College, the second-largest granite building in the world, I finally caught up with King Robert the Bruce at a time when he was beginning at last to exert some control over his kingdom: riding aloft on horseback, holding a charter with his left hand. In 1319, he established a Common Good Fund which benefits the citizens of Aberdeen to this day.

Union Street is Aberdeen's great thoroughfare, built in 1801 almost entirely of granite to celebrate the union of Britain and Ireland. Although having completely disappeared now, Aberdeen Castle was located at the east end of what is now Union Street, in the Castlegait area. The town's citizens helped Bruce's forces capture the fortress in 1308. The password to begin the attack, 'bon accord', meaning 'good agreement', thereafter became the city's motto.

CHAPTER 7

Deeside to Forfar

REACHING ABERDEEN, I was 1,000km (600miles) into my journey. Bruce had quelled his Scottish opposition and I had quelled the doubts and insecurities that had nearly derailed me at the start of the walk. The longer the walk went on the stronger I felt and the more accustomed I became to this nomadic lifestyle. I bobbed along Union Street, pleased with my little milestone and looking forward with gusto, not apprehension, to the second stage of my walk: seeking out the significant places and events of Bruce's reign after 1308. With his main Scottish enemies defeated, he now turned to wrenching the country back from the control of King Edward II and re-establishing a fully functioning, independent realm, properly recognised by the international powers of the day. No small task, more than any of his predecessors had achieved. In 1308, the odds of realising these ambitions were in the magnitude of thousands to one. Even united,

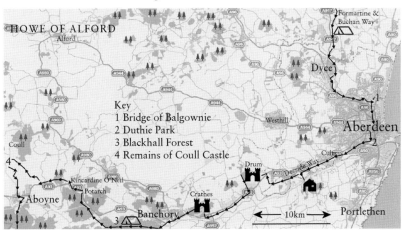

Aberdeen and the Deeside Way.

147

Scotland was a small, poor nation when compared to the power and wealth of England, one of the strongest of medieval European kingdoms. Remembering also that the country had been riven by war for 12 years and was still garrisoned by Edward II's troops, the turnaround in fortunes engineered by Bruce was nothing short of astonishing. Trying to pack this into the second part of my walk, I would be compressing a period of over 20 years into a little over three weeks. By making use of the best available walking routes, I intended to travel down the eastern side of the country, crossing the border to reach Berwick upon Tweed before turning around and heading back via the Scottish Borders towards Stirling to finish at Bannockburn.

With the north and the west of Scotland now under control and almost free (Banff Castle being the exception) of any occupying forces, Bruce began to attack further south, in the knowledge that he could focus on his enemies whilst his rear and flanks were secure – no decent general wants a war on two fronts. I was aiming for Forfar Castle as Bruce rolled out his programme of guerrilla warfare into Angus. The best route south was along an ancient highway, although I would have to deviate inland to catch up with it. This would give me opportunity to investigate a couple of legends en route.

A short hop from Union Street was Duthie Park, 44 acres of restored parkland on the banks of the River Dee, Aberdeen's other encompassing river. The heavens opened as I arrived, so without lingering, I climbed aboard the Deeside Way, another of Scotland's Great Trails. This former railway line, made into an all abilities path, runs from the heart of Aberdeen to the countryside of Aberdeenshire.

Carrying only the bare essentials is surely the key to getting the most enjoyment out of a long distance walk. By keeping my pack weight down, I could reduce the pain and strain on my shoulders and back, thereby increasing my morale and the distance I could travel each day. However, I had allowed myself the luxury of a lightweight umbrella as recommended by Ray Jardine, the great promoter of lightweight backpacking. The other tip I had picked up from his book *Trail Life* was to wear shoes rather than boots. This hadn't worked out well: my shoes were nowhere near as comfortable as boots and any weight

A birch-lined path on the Deeside Way.

advantage gained was negated by the extra pain endured. There were many days when my feet were extremely painful, causing me to hobble awkwardly. Blisters just kept cropping up in new places. There are a lot of entries in my travel journal complaining about painful toes, worn heels and septic soles.

Anyway, back to umbrellas – being able to keep the rain at bay as well as being able to keep my head up and look around prevented morale from going down the pan during sustained wet periods. It was just a pity that in Scotland, rain and wind normally go hand in hand, so it was a practical accessory only rarely. On this occasion, I was sheltered from the wind by the surrounding greenery and managed to wedge the shaft of the umbrella under a shoulder strap, with the parasol section leaning on the top of the rucksack. I could walk with my umbrella up, hands free. I must have looked like Inspector Gadget, so when anyone passed by and to prevent outbursts of mirth, I put up my hand to pretend I was hanging on to it.

The path provided an express route out of the city, at a height level with the upstairs windows of the passing houses – like Chicago's high riding metro rail system, although the similarity ends there. Leaving the city, I passed through former stations, such as Cults, Murtle, Bieldside and Culter.

At Milltimber, I crossed the River Dee to reach a Holiday Park at Maryculter, arriving just before the office shut for the evening. It was £15 to camp, or £35 for a luxury camping hut and with the rain still teeming down it was easy to be persuaded to upgrade. On the way over to the cylindrical pods, which were nicely grouped overlooking a duck pond, my legs buckled and exhaustion hit me like a blow to the head. Closing the door on the elements, I switched on the electric heating and collapsed on a wonderful mattress, arms and legs spread out, floating in sheer delirium. Later, in the campsite kitchen, I began heating my super noodles, almost the last of my rations. Whilst speaking to a guy from Liverpool – who was working at a local care home and living in a small tent – I spilled the pan of noodles and boiling water over my legs. I pulled the trouser fabric off my skin and stood staring at my last meal swimming on the floor. My head was numb, my thighs seared. The guy could see the look of shock on my face. 'Pick them up, they will be alright,' he said. I did. I had no choice, I was starving and had nothing else hot but porridge. Soon I returned to my hut and sorted out my gear. During the wee small hours, walking to the toilet block in the still torrential rain, I thought the maintenance man needed a rocket up his backside; there were numerous flickering bulbs needing replaced – I hadn't realised it was flashes of lightning, such was my exhaustion.

If ever I had picked a good evening not to be under canvas that was it. I said goodbye to the ecstatic ducks and headed back onto the Deeside Way, feeling refreshed. At Coalford, I left the old railway line once more and followed a minor road and then an overgrown track to Drum Castle. (When is a shortcut never a shortcut? Almost always!) Occupied by the Irvines for over 600 years, this castle with a large, 13th-century tower, is now in the care of the National Trust for Scotland. William de Irvine came here in 1323 and the legend relates

Drum Castle and the 13th-century hunting tower.

that he was given the lands, including the hunting tower, in gratitude for helping Robert the Bruce during his wanderings of 1306–07. In fact he was reputed to have hidden Bruce under a holly bush, to help him avoid capture. I was keen to find out if I could add another name to Bruce's band of heroic lieutenants.

The true story was less dramatic. William de Irvine was an able clerk who was sent to the area as a keeper of part of the royal forest of Drum; he was also a collector of taxes and would have sought to bring stronger governance to the area. The holly leaf in the insignia of the Irvines denoted him as a keeper of the royal forest. Furthermore, had he helped the King during his darkest days, Bruce would have put on the royal charters to William de Irvine, of which there are two, 'for homage and services given', which he did not.[24]

I chatted to Penny, one of the volunteer guides, who told me that within the ancient walls a medieval chamber had just been discovered. Previously hidden for hundreds of years and complete with its own garderobe, this was surely the hideout for Irvine of Drum who in 1746 after the Battle of Culloden evaded capture for three years. Penny said she preferred Bruce to Wallace, as Bruce united the country like no other. Although Wallace and Bruce are often mentioned in the same sentence, people usually have a personal preference for one or the other. Wallace who never gave up his ideals, a warrior who fought like a tiger, inspired a nation and found fame in martyrdom. Bruce, of noble lineage, who took a more flexible approach to achieving his objectives, but became a consistent applicant of the rules of war and governance he developed over 20 years.

I left Drum Estate by the rear entrance. In a nearby field filled with sheep and lambs, a buzzard swooped down and started tearing away at something on the ground, probably an afterbirth. Seeing the bird chomping away reminded me of my hunger – I still had no provisions, nor pound notes to buy anything from the local shop, where plastic was anathema. I hurried a few kilometres along the Deeside Way to Crathes Castle where there was a café which would hopefully take my bank card. With turrets and towers protruding from every corner and its pink harl, tall, narrow Crathes was a real fairy-tale castle. For a change, though, it wasn't the castle I was here to see. Hanging above the fireplace in the great hall on the second floor was the Horn of Leys, a bejewelled, ivory hunting horn. The knowledgeable and enthusiastic guide explained that the horn, made from a hollowed tusk, probably came from a wart hog as it was too curly for a wild boar. Although the horn didn't turn up in family inventories until the 19th century, the Burnetts have had a hunting horn in their crest since the 1500s and this horn's style is consistent with Bruce's time. The legend goes that when Alexander Burnard (Burnett) was appointed a keeper of part of the royal forest of Drum in 1323, Bruce gifted him the horn. I would have loved to have had a toot on the instrument, but legend goes that when the horn is blown someone from the family dies.

Originally, the Burnett family lived on a crannog in the now drained Loch of Leys; Crathes Castle itself was built in the 16th century and is justifiably famous for its painted ceilings, but I just had time for a quick squint at them using a hand-held mirror. I had an appointment with some food at the café. Just as I sat down with my sausage roll and beans, Meg found an audience. A family took interest in the dog and I was chewing on my fist in between answering questions about Robert

A not so wild campsite and Meg resting comfortably.

the flaming Bruce whilst staring at my rapidly cooling lunch.

I descended through the woods towards Banchory and came across a gigantic Tesco, where I restocked, carefully this time. Crossing the Dee at Deer Street, near the centre of the town, I headed into the Blackhall Forest to camp for the evening.

In the middle of the night a stag crept up to the tent and began roaring its lungs out. I bolted upright and looked at Meg, who, having sat up equally quickly, just stared back at me, confoundingly silent. Unfortunately, I didn't have a command for her to *bark like hell*. It was a frightening racket and I could only imagine the size of the monster that could bellow like that. Then it all went quiet outside before I heard the roaring again, but further away. I lay back down and just as my heart rate was returning to normal, it roared again, right outside the tent – the angry beast must have been taking a run up, and I waited for a set of antlers to come piercing through the flimsy fabric! The worst didn't happen, so I started whispering to Meg, 'Bark! Bark!'. She had gone mute, so I had to bark myself. The beast must have wandered off thinking that this black triangle wasn't providing much sport. Eventually I stuck my head out of the tent, but my head torch hardly penetrated the pitch dark of the forest. I didn't want to instigate any more trouble, so I lay back down. It took me a right long while to get back to sleep after that.

I began my 43rd day by searching unsuccessfully for giant cloven hoof prints, then hiked along a network of paths through coniferous forest and out onto General Wade's road. Alongside the now tarmacked road, a path runs downhill through Slewdrum Forest to Potarch. This area of open parkland, toilets and benches is perfect for a family day out and I pictured my girls practising their gymnastics on the grass, while Nicola relaxed with a glass of wine and the dogs and I ate all the leftover sandwiches. At the River Dee, I got a chance to dispel my daydreams as I chatted to an outdoor instructor and watched his charges, novice kayakers, negotiate a short stretch of rapids and paddle under the handsome, three-arched Telford Bridge. Once again following the course of the river, I headed for Kincardine O'Neil, where on the outskirts of the village and within an old graveyard lay 14th-century St Marys Kirk. In use for over 500 years, today it stands roofless, as it was in 1733 when the thatch was set alight by a villager shooting at a pigeon perched on the roof – thereafter, it was slated. No one was around. No one hangs around kirkyards, but historically, fairs were held here. In 1777, a petition was raised to move the fairs because 'stealing, brawling, fighting and every indecency took place within the shade of the church'. Kincardine O'Neil, the oldest village on Deeside, is where the first bridge across the river was situated. It was here, in 1296, that Edward 1's triumphant army crossed the Dee and rested one night, leaving neither 'maut nor ale'.[25]

I said a final goodbye to the Deeside Way at Boddomend Farm and headed uphill on a pink stone path bordered with yellow flowering gorse, towards ruined farm buildings at Bonnyside. From there, an ever-fainter path took me into the conifer plantations on Mortlich Hill, one of the eastern guardians of a low lying and flat area called the Howe of Cromar. On the other side of this fertile basin lie the Cairngorm Mountains.

Below me, at a tiny hamlet, were the remains of a major fortification.

I walked down past Gallow Hill, where local justice was meted out, to Coull Castle. This large fortress was built by the Durward family in the 13th century, their chief seat amongst their vast lands, which had been part of the Earldom of Mar, but by 1308 was in the hands of the English Crown. En route, I walked past the 18th-century kirk built atop an older religious establishment – the castle and the kirk being the old centres of civic life in the community – and onto the field where the ruined castle lay under grass. Only fragments of stone bely the fact that one of Scotland's best 13th-century fortresses lies underneath. An excavation in 1923 by WD Simpson revealed that the castle featured a pentagonal courtyard and the curtain walls were augmented by five towers. On one side, the castle was protected by the Tarland Burn. Ditches were hewn out of the rock on the other sides to further augment its defences. Its relatively short life was ended by Robert the Bruce in 1308 after a lengthy siege (the sewers were found to be solid with waste). The castle's end was met when the walls and towers were undermined and the whole building set ablaze, a towering inferno signalling to the local people (among whom fire was a powerful signal and superstitious force), that King Robert had vanquished his foes and reigned unchallenged in the northeast.[26]

The Howe of Cromar seemed to be a hidden gem, a beautiful little flat and prosperous hollow, protected by hills and mountains on three sides and the River Dee to the south. The shouts and screams of the dying, the wailing of the bereaved, the destruction and burning that took place here has been swallowed up by 700 years of tranquillity. I wished I could have explored further but as usual I had to push on.

A new footpath, the Tarland Way, follows the Tarland Burn south into the village of Aboyne. Here begins the famous route through the hills, which would take me eventually to Forfar. I had completed my journeying in the northeast; like Bruce, I could move on knowing my job was done. Before leaving the tarmac, I rested at the huge triangular Green of Charlestown, where annual Highland Games are held.

The route south is known as the Fungle – variously described as an ancient highway, a smugglers' path and a drove road. It was all three at one time or another and one of the main routes through the mountains

The Fungle Road, a route through the hills for hundreds of years.

in bygone days. Passing the Boat Inn, I crossed the Dee for the last time and headed onto the Fungle Road, which was overhung with trees as it followed the bank of the Allt Dinnhe steeply uphill before passing between Birsemore Hill and Craigendinnie. It was after 8pm by the time I reached the top of the pass, so I thought I would be causing a minimum amount of disturbance by stopping overnight at the Rest and be Thankful, where a small platform of grass encompassed by a low stone dyke was perfect for camping, sitting, cooking and contemplating the views.

The weather was beautiful as I set out the next day and I began by walking through a picturesque natural woodland where I crossed the Alt Dinnhe once more. I tried to encourage Meg to drink from the stream, thinking it would be a while before we came across water again. 'Take a drink! Go on, take a drink!' I cried, like a drunk trying to convince an abstainer to partake of his poison. Meg just stared

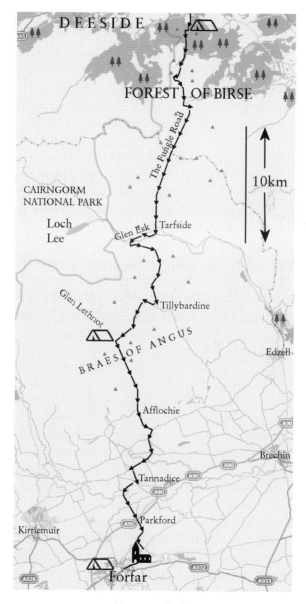

Aboyne to Forfar.

back, head tilted, one ear cocked.

The morning's walking felt like a perfectly imagined Highland scene: following a riverside path alongside gurgling waters, stepping lightly on muddy clay, surrounded by purple heather, yellow gorse, golden bracken and scattered Scots pines to emerge onto heather-clad moorland. Meadow pipits flitted lightly and snow-capped peaks shone brightly under an azure sky. Over hundreds of years, the only thing that had changed was the dress of the humans who passed by.

Passing below the tops of Carnferg and Brackenstake and round a big bend in the path, I climbed up to the only blot on the landscape, a private bothy, before passing below the Hill of Duchery to descend alongside the Gwaves, a deeply cut channel, towards Birse Castle. Crossing the head of the valley, where the restored castle sits, I followed the Water of Feuch south towards its source. Gleefully, I watched some leverets scampering around, playing with their siblings; they were easily spotted on their playground of burnt heather. The mother, whose coat was part winter white, part summer fawn, stood on her hind legs surveying for danger. Puggled by the heat, I trudged uphill. This was really hard going! At a height of 600m I reached the Slochd, a bealach between the hills of Mudlee Bracks and Tampie.

On the descent I left Aberdeenshire and entered the old county of Forfarshire, now renamed Angus. The hillside is used for the rearing and despatch of grouse. Halfway down, on a beauty-spoiling gravel road, a gamekeeper came zooming uphill, stopped his Land Rover Defender and asked that I keep Meg off the heather as she would frighten the mothers into abandoning their offspring. Sulking, I kept her to heel as I continued onwards, the gamie keeping me within sight. Walking through fields surrounding the old hill farm of Shinfur, I was dive-bombed by some noisy lapwings protecting their nests, rolling, climbing steeply and performing banking turns. Their aerial displays were distracting and soon stemmed my annoyance. At the meeting of the Burn of Tennet and the Water of Tarf, I sat on the rocks beside the now bulked-up river and had my usual lunchtime fare, made fabulous by the natural and peaceful setting. Feeling dozy from a combination of the heat and over-eating, I forced myself onwards through the fields,

Restenneth Priory, burial place of one of Bruce's sons.

eyes half shut, with only the shrill cries of oyster catchers and curlews breaking through my partial shutdown.

Reaching the hamlet of Tarfside in Glen Esk, I needed to cross the River North Esk to continue south. A sign by the footpath said that the footbridge was closed, but to avoid a detour I gingerly crossed it anyway, only to find the far side impassable due to a locked gate bristling with barbed wire. I retreated back across the supposedly unsafe bridge and followed the river west, towards a ford that was marked on my old map. On the way I met a local resident who thought it would be impractical because of recent rains and when I arrived at the crossing, her theory was proved right. The overgrown track approaching the water suggested the ford had not been used for a long time. Nor could I tell how deep the water was and it looked a mite fast-flowing for Meg and my electrical gadgets. I wimped out and continued up the glen for a couple of kilometres to Dalbrack, where there was a sturdy bridge. Hurrying to make up for lost time, I followed an old, disused track round the north flank of Garlet Hill. A combination of the physical exertion and spluttering red grouse kept my heart beating furiously. At a bealach shared with Cowie Hill, a new hill track continued along the side of West Knock Hill; these new access roads were a blot on the landscape but did make for fast going. Soon enough I was descending to Tillybardine Farm at Glen Lethnot.

As I headed west on the public road, a herd of Highland cattle I'd heard thundering back and forth on the brae above, all of a sudden thundered downhill in front of me. Half of them then charged back up the hill, the other half stayed where they were. Meg and I had managed to split the pack! Just as we were about to pass between the two halves, they charged from either side in a classic pincer movement. I retreated and they congregated in front of us, big horns menacingly pointing, lots of snorting and moist breath exhaled. Unnerved by their behaviour, I whooped and cried, whirled my sticks like a champion majorette and strode forwards with Meg at my side. The menacing Red Sea parted and I felt the warm breath as I ran through the gap, Meg bravely sticking by my side. What a trusting companion she is.

I camped at the end of the public road and sat taking notes and looking up tranquil Glen Lethnot towards the Cairngorm National Park. Next morning I crossed the Water of Sauchs at Waterhead, passing farm and estate buildings. With loose bowels, I walked on a faint, southwesterly path gradually climbing the Hill of Monduran, all the while telling my bum to hold on. All civilisation out of sight, I found blessed relief. In a far more relaxed and unclenched state, I continued round the head of a small valley and down a shoulder of Hill of Garbet, past grouse-shooting butts and dipped

Forfar Castle was sited on this hilltop in the centre of town.

down to little Glen Cruick. Emerging from the hills at Afflochie, I followed minor roads south, crossing the dual carriageway of the A90 at Bogindollo farm, eventually reaching Restenneth Priory.

I hoped this would be an undiscovered gem relating to Bruce, although its former dramatic setting was destroyed when the surrounding loch was drained. Of the ruins, an ancient tower remains intact and some of the choir walls with lancet windows remain at full height, but overall it was a disappointment. There has been a lack of archaeological work undertaken here and there is minimal explanation of the above ground remains and of the history. Prior to the Wars of Independence, the area was patronised by Scottish monarchs and during the troubles, national records from Jedburgh Abbey were brought here for safekeeping. This may have brought extra attention to the church; it is recorded that the church was burned and that records were destroyed or removed during the long period of strife. Later, Robert the Bruce became a benefactor to the church and there must have been a connection between the King and Restenneth because his infant son, John, was interred here in 1327. John was a twin of David who eventually acceded the throne as David II in 1329. Imagine the consternation that twins would have caused in claiming the throne.[27]

At the end of the day I reached the town of Forfar, a Royal Burgh which grew in part due to the time spent here by Scottish monarchs from the time of Malcolm Canmore to Alexander III. It occupies a central place in the early history of the country, witnessing conflicts between Picts and Scots, and Scots and Danes. As the shops were closing up, I headed through the streets to a town-centre campsite beside the Loch of Forfar. In 1296, Edward I called the town 'une bonne ville', maybe because it was rebuilt after an accidental fire in 1244.

The next morning, after collecting a key from the newsagent on Castle Street, I walked round the corner, unlocked the concertina type gate and climbed up the steps to the site of Forfar Castle. Situated on a large mound, the castle had been an extensive building, important enough to feature as the town's symbol on the old burgh seals. It was protected by a moat and by the Loch of Forfar which, prior to the level being lowered, extended to the foot of Castle Hill. In 1308, the castle was subject to a night attack by Scottish forces, who were led by Philip 'the forester of Plater'. Using ladders, access was gained to the battlements and the main gate was opened to allow the greater part of the patriot's force to enter. The English garrison, once overcome, were slain. The castle was the first captured south of the mountains. Although it was not a major stronghold, this would have announced the beginning of upheaval in this area. Coming upon the back of the Herschip of Buchan, it would have focused the 'hearts and minds' of local people. Nothing of the castle remains and it may never have been rebuilt after it was cast down upon the orders of Robert the Bruce. Ruins were in evidence until the 19th century and doubtless stone from the fort was used in buildings of the town. The top of Castle Hill is now an enclosed garden filled with trees. In the centre stands a 6.5m tall stone tower which was the town's 17th-century mercat cross, rebuilt on the hill in 1785 and accessed by metal steps. Weathered carvings are just visible at the top of the tower, from which the surrounding area can be surveyed.[28]

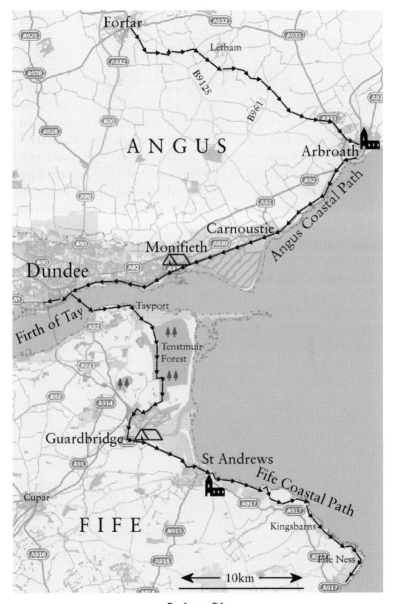

Forfar to Fife.

CHAPTER 8

The Fife Coastal Path

LEAVING FORFAR, I headed for Arbroath, on the Angus coast. Not far to the south of the town, at Cauldhame, I was walking alongside some woodland when the undergrowth rustled and an elderly man sporting a deerstalker and followed by two black labradors broke out from the trees.

'I saw you on the telly last night,' he cried. I nearly jumped out of my skin.

Delighted that my interview had made the news, I knew damn fine how he had recognised me, so I didn't ask. I chatted away with the gamekeeper about dogs. Robert the Bruce didn't come into it.

The back roads were busier with commercial traffic than I anticipated and the verges were non-existent: I was hopping on and off the road a lot. At Dunnichen, I took a breather beside a replica Pictish symbol stone. The original was found on the slopes of Dunnichen Hill and is contemporary with the nearby Battle of Nechtansmere, where in 685AD the Picts won a vital victory against Northumbrian incursion. Thereafter, the Picts reclaimed lost ground and their southern border once more became the River Forth. It was a dreich day, brightened only by the thought of two Forfar bridies gently warming in my breast pocket. After lunch and a determined afternoon push, I was on the outskirts of Arbroath when a couple stopped their car to ask a question that had been bugging them since my interview had been broadcast on STV North the previous evening: My wife wants to know, 'does Meg really carry her pyjamas in that rucksack?'

I needn't have bothered following in the footsteps of the famous King. I could have just trailed round the country with the dog. No one cared about Robert the Bruce, it's Meg the border collie that people wanted to know about.

Located in the middle of Arbroath, the largest town in Angus,

Arbroath Abbey with its repaired 'Round O' window to the left of the picture.

were the magnificent red sandstone ruins of Arbroath Abbey. More important to me was the visitor centre, where I headed to escape the elements. Meg and I were warmly welcomed by the staff.

The abbey was founded in 1178 by King William the Lyon and the great church became the centre of a prosperous religious order. There were many buildings within the walled community of Tironesian monks, each of whom had to learn a trade to help develop the abbeys resources. The great church was built in 55 years, quickly for a church of this size. When complete, it was covered in lime wash, making it an object of awe and place of pilgrimage. High up in the south transept remains a circular window, known as 'the Round O', behind which a fire was lit by the monks to provide a navigational aid for mariners. Funnily enough, it was one of the great lighthouse-building family, the Stevensons, who repaired the damaged window in the 19th century and gave Arbroath its famous symbol back. Nationally and internationally, Arbroath is most famous for the declaration made by the Scottish nobles to Pope John XXII in 1320. Written in the lay section of the abbey by Abbot Bernard de Linton, with the seals of many leading

Scottish nobles attached, it hoped to achieve what success on the field of battle had failed to provide – freedom from English intervention in Scotland and recognition of Robert the Bruce as rightful King of Scots.

The Scots nobles stated that they would defy English overlordship to the last and would oust Robert the Bruce if he wavered from that cause. In a way, they were backdating support for and attempting to legitimise Bruce's seizure of the throne 14 years earlier. King John Balliol, who had accepted English overlordship, was still alive and a crowned King of Scots when Bruce supplanted him. At the time of the declaration Robert was excommunicated by the Pope for having refused Papal letters in 1317 and for not accepting a proposed truce with England. The document has become world famous as an expression of national freedom; in 1998 the US government stated that their own Declaration of Independence of 1776 had been modelled on the Declaration of Arbroath.

Andrew, one of the members of Historic Scotland's staff, explained that the abbey's connection with Robert the Bruce did not end there – in 1318 Bruce appointed the very first Lyon, King of Arms, here at Arbroath. The position exists to this day and the Lord Lyon is responsible for all matters of Heraldry in Scotland. I had my own experience of this office when Clan Ewing decided to appoint a chief after an absence of 500 years. In order to elect a leader, the clan held a derbhfine: this ancient method of selecting a chief was a lot simpler and more authentic than the alternative, a lengthy and expensive legal process. Traditionally, the derbhfine was a meeting of the leading men of the family. In 2014, men and women attending the annual gathering of the clan, raised their hands and said 'Aye' in support of John Thor Ewing. He was thus elected Clan Commander and if he successfully represents the interests of Clan Ewing, then he will be elected chief in five years' time. A representative of the Lord Lyon was at the Derbhfine to ensure its legitimacy and he duly reported back to his boss.

Delighted with the history, distraught with the weather, I continued through the windswept streets to the harbour, where I picked up the Angus Coastal Path. At a beach shelter I cooked and ate, watching the dog walkers being blown past me. Continuing on through Elliot Links, an area of vegetation-covered sand dunes, I camped near Easthaven in a dip which provided at least a little shelter from the squalls. It was a long rough night, but with battery power to spare, I listened to some podcasts on my phone, attempting to drown out the sound of the raging storm whilst nervously munching my way through the remains of my rations.

I awoke in a partially collapsed tent, so I didn't dilly dally around; the cold was intense as I packed up, but the wind at least had lost some of its vehemence. The public toilets in the little community of Easthaven were a godsend, providing fresh water and shelter. I sat in a cold stall and made some repairs to my tortured feet, a regular chore that had been forgotten about during the previous night's storm.

On a sandy beach I sought a sheltered recess amongst the dunes to prepare breakfast. The cold had penetrated right through my body. Once porridge and coffee had stoked the fires of my inner core, I continued along the beach to Carnoustie Golf Links, home of the Open Championship on seven occasions. The army had cornered off a promontory at Barry Links and so I followed the path inland, through the golf course and then alongside the army base, accompanied by the incessant chatter from the rifle range.

At Monifieth I checked into a campsite, spruced up and then headed into the village. The Crown Inn looked like a relaxing and sheltered place to while away an afternoon off. Coke and salted peanuts were my sustenance as I sat watching world championship snooker. The pub banter was mainly concerned with acquiring tickets for Dundee FC's final match of the season against Dumbarton, when a win would guarantee promotion to the Premier League. Catching up on emails, I received word that the VAT man was looking for me and didn't want to wait until I returned home to get the answers he was looking for. I tried to recall some of the information that the impatient tax collector might be after, but all this stuff was locked in a compartment in my brain, the key to which had been thrown away weeks ago. I made the call anyway and thought the worst when I got a heavy-handed dressing down, but once my pursuer had got that out of his system, I pleaded my unavailability and he relented, giving me the time required to send the information to him. Phew!

Lunchtime on Saturday 3 May found me at the city of Dundee, having walked along the shoreline of the Firth of Tay, past the affluent suburb of Broughty Ferry. The copious amount of reconstruction around the waterfront signified the beginnings of a belated renaissance for the city, hopefully something like which Glasgow experienced in the 1980s and from which it has never looked back. Along with the improved infrastructure, hotels and visitor attractions, undoubtedly the highest profile arrival will be the forthcoming Victorian and Albert Museum of Design.

On the site of Dundee Castle stands St Paul's Cathedral. Bruce captured Dundee in March or April 1312 and the castle was probably demolished at that time; there are no details of the engagement but we do know that at approximately the same time a parliament was held at Inchture, just a few miles along the road towards Perth (which was still in English hands). Between 1308 and his capture of Dundee, Bruce had continued to extend his authority in Scotland. The only attempts made by Edward II to directly counter this was an incursion in 1310–11 which, despite provocation, did not tempt Bruce to discard his guerrilla tactics and fight in a pitched battle. Failing to find Scots to fight or food to eat, the English army retreated, having accomplished nothing.

I crossed the 2.25km Tay Bridge, with its sympathetic low-to-the-

Looking back over the Tay to Dundee.

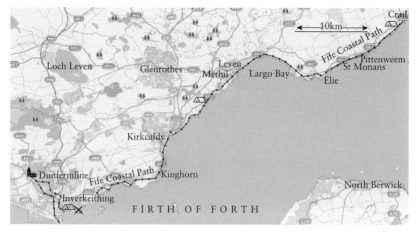

The Fife Coastal Path.

water style of construction that did not dominate the Firth of Tay – letting the surrounding views do the talking. Pedestrians use the centre aisle, with cars flying by on either side. The views back towards Dundee were visitor-welcoming: Captain Scott's ship *Discovery* lying off to port side and the city climbing uphill towards its green crown, The Law.

Returning to earth I entered the kingdom of Fife, heading for the medieval town of St Andrews. I would be following another of Scotland's Great Trails, the Fife Coastal Path. Fife is a peninsula of land squeezed between the Tay, the Forth, the Ochil Hills and the North Sea – natural and protective borders which made Fife a kingdom within a kingdom. The prominence of the area was recognised by the fact that the Earls of Fife were held to be the most senior of Scotland's original seven earls. During the inauguration of a new monarch, the honour of placing the crown upon the King of Scots' head was given to them.

A raised path allowed views across the Tay Estuary to the ground I had covered that morning. At Tayport the path weaved alongside back gardens before dropping down to the harbour and continuing along the shore past WWII coastal defences. I took a shortcut through Tentsmuir Forest; it was nice to escape civilisation for a while. Coming out near Leuchars Airfield, I walked along the perimeter fence looking for weak spots. Just after Guardbridge, I camped for the evening, watching birds, not planes, fly low along the Eden Estuary.

It seemed appropriate to be walking into Saint Andrews, the long-time religious capital of Scotland, on a Sunday morning. Formerly, the most prominent religion was the Catholic Church. Nowadays, Sunday morning instruction is just as often taken in golf. Shrill cries from the Strathtyrum course had me peering over the high hedge where a female was crying into her partner's chest as he awkwardly patted her back. It seemed rude to intrude, surely such devastation couldn't be golf related?

On the outskirts of Saint Andrews, I was mystified by the Arabian looking Old Course Hotel, temple-shaped and sand-coloured. From the 18th tee of the Old Course, the view was more familiar: I looked down the fairway to the ancient, humpbacked Swilcan Bridge, which would undoubtedly have been crossed by Bruce, but made famous by Jack Nicklaus waving farewell to the gantries in 2005. The wealth of this new religion was easily comparable to that of the old Catholic Church; where else in Scotland would you get two Bentleys parked behind one another in a public street? Absorbed by my surroundings, I sat by the bandstand in front of the Martyrs Monument which is devoted to those who dared to complain at the trappings of the old Church. This area, known as the Bow Butts, was where Scots fulfilled their legal obligation to partake of archery.

The morning was warming nicely and the town was yet to come to life when I heard captivating, medieval sounds from the Chapel of St Salvator at the heart of the University of St Andrews. Beautiful, high pitched, joyous choral music percolated along the quiet streets. The old religion wasn't giving in without a fight; I was tempted to run in and confess on the spot.

It was an earlier incarnation of Saint Andrews Castle that existed in Bruce's time; the current remains are mainly from the 16th century and the castle's most famous features are a mine and burrowing counter mine that date from 1546AD. I crept down the latter as it delved into the earth; hastily dug, its purpose was to intercept the tunnel that

St Andrews Cathedral, the religious centre of medieval Scotland.

the besiegers were scooping out to undermine the castle walls. I imagined a ferocious battle taking place when the opposing miners eventually met. Swinging pickaxes, the blood and yells from combat at close quarters, I could see it all – then suddenly, a bus-load of Japanese tourists came charging down the narrow passageway in a state of high excitement, their lack of height being a definite advantage – and I snapped back to reality.

Within sight of the castle are the remains of St Andrews Cathedral, which after 158 years of building work was finally consecrated in 1318. The largest church in Scotland and home to the venerated remains of Andrew the Apostle, it became a mecca for pilgrims. After the Reformation it was dismantled as an easy quarry for local builders and there are only just enough graceful ruins to allow an appreciation of what this great cathedral was once like. Strangely, the tower of the previous church, St Rules, stands intact. Climbing the 143 steps gave me a lofty view of the surrounding plain.

In March 1309, Bruce held his first parliament in the as yet unfinished cathedral. A significant proportion of the clergy, nobles and communities of Scotland attended and gave their support to him as the rightfully entitled King of Scots. Such strong backing on a national scale from all three estates of the realm must have been deeply satisfying: it demonstrated how far Bruce had come in only two years.

The beautifully constructed but badly named St Andrews Sarcophagus is housed in the cathedral visitor centre and is one of the finest examples of early medieval sculpture in Europe. Spectacularly carved, it features uniquely Pictish images as well as scenes of biblical Kings. An 8th-century shrine from a long-forgotten church, it lay buried for

The St Andrews Sarcophagus.

1,000 years under the feet of Edward I, Robert the Bruce and most crucially of all, the Protestant reformers. It was exciting to behold and a bit of rebranding is long overdue. Scotland's very own ark, conceivably it could have contained anything your imagination would like to come up with.

I left St Andrews by the quiet harbour and marched purposefully under the historic walls, along the busy path behind East Sands beach, overtaking lovers, strollers and fellow dog walkers. I had a long way to go before my evening camp. The walking was scenic and varied as I hurried along below cliffs, up and down crisscrossed stone steps, following footsteps on sandy beaches, discovering deserted coves and unspoiled inlets as I went. From a distance, I looked back to St Andrews. The towering ruins still make a commanding spectacle. In a 14th-century world, the completed cathedral must have been a mind-blowing sight to the arriving pilgrims.

Only briefly did the path head inland at Boarhills Farm, other than that, the coastal walking continued to be exhilarating with more golden sands to stir happy childhood memories and provide a cushioned platform for aching feet. At Kingsbarns the path skirted along the golf course, but the ladies and gents were on form and there were no shouts of single digit numbers. Constantine's Cave was, according to local legend, where the 9th-century Scots King Constantine was killed after being defeated by marauding Vikings. Had it not been in the midst of Balcomie Links Golf Course then it would have been a great and atmospheric place to spend the night. At Fife Ness, the most easterly point in Fife, cormorants, eider ducks, fulmars and twitchers gathered by an ancient tide mill. Nearby Kilminning Castle has no connections with the Bruce, being an entirely natural rock formation protruding from the coastline, which the RAF targeted with bags of flour during bombing practice in WWII.

The beautiful village of Crail has been trading salt and fish internationally since people were praying at the St Andrews Sarcophagus. Created a Royal Burgh in 1310 by Robert the Bruce (he also allowed Sunday trading), it retains much of its historic character with its narrow streets and 12th-century parish church. A walkway skirts round the site of an ancient royal castle, remains of which there are none; this leads to a viewpoint overlooking the neat, 16th-century harbour.

On the Fife Coastal Path.

The village of Crail's brightly coloured roofs were a symbol of foreign trade.

Out in the Firth of Forth, as the eyes scan from left to right, there are three prominent protrusions: the Isle of May, once harbouring monks; the Bass Rock, an ancient prison; and North Berwick Law, topped by a whale's jawbone.

Crail is just one of the beautifully unspoiled villages in the East Neuk of Fife. The former wealth of these communities is reflected in the fact that there were no less than six royal burghs created in a short section of coastline. The harbours of each village allowed fishing and trading to flourish and they reached their prime in the 16th and 17th centuries when Scotland's trading focus was the Low Countries. After the Union with England, Scotland gained new markets and lost others. Glasgow and the west coast towns thrived – the east coast lost out. The industrial revolution also missed out these villages and they have retained the character of their heyday. A reminder of ancient trading partners was all around: the bright orange pan tile roof slates on many of the older houses came from the Low Countries, probably as ship's ballast.

After resting on the sloped parkland between the town and the beach I carried on just a bit farther along the coast and camped at The Pans – a lovely spot with the added shelter of a ruined cottage. At dusk, sitting on a log sipping coffee, I looked out to the empty sea. When the contentment gained from a satisfying day's walking wore off, the cold and the loneliness made poor companions and chased me to bed.

An early morning jogger woke Meg, Meg woke me, so at 6am I was sitting on my log once more, this time watching little boats collecting pots from the shallows. A good track along the shore, took me past a series of caves hollowed out of the sandstone cliffs by the sea that have at one time or another been home to Christians, hermits, livestock and, as I discovered when I had a nosey inside, some furiously flapping bats. Near to Cellardyke a majestic buzzard, oblivious to my presence, was sitting on a fence post, patiently watching the seabirds frolicking on the rocks. On the outskirts of the village, the public toilets were closed so I rushed on past the empty harbour and through the narrow streets to Anstruther, the largest community of the East Neuk. A tourist destination, there were shops aplenty, the harbour was busy with queues for boat trips and the toilets were open. Watching the comings and goings, I spoke to Alfie from Dyce who was walking the Fife Coastal Path in the opposite direction to me. He had been in the oil business and had lived in Tehran before the Iranian Revolution. His bosses had suggested he should move to Dubai the year before the uprising, so he didn't have the drama of the Americans in Ben Affleck's *Argo* but he had really liked everything about Tehran, including the drives out to the Caspian Sea.

I crossed the Dreel Burn, which splits Anstruther into two communities: Easter and Wester, both of which were Royal Burghs. Wester Anstruther Parish Church was the oldest building I came across, which despite extensive remodelling was dated to at least the 17th century, but mooted to be 300 years older.

The villages were coming thick and fast: next up was Pittenweem followed by St Monans, where there were the remains of 18th-century industry – saltpans, once powered by a Dutch-looking windmill. St Monans was also a pretty village and the planted wellies were unusual, but I was becoming numb to crow-stepped gables. Perched almost in the sea was St Monans Church, built by David II in thanks for deliverance from a particularly rough crossing of the Firth of Forth. I met an Australian couple who were visiting the remains of Newark Castle which they believed their ancestors, the Sandilands, had built.

A happy couple at Elie Scarecrow Festival.

Further along the path, there was even less remaining of Ardross Castle. Neither of the ruins had interpretation boards, so I couldn't project myself into the past to conjure up images of people or events.

The combined villages of Elie and Earlsferry offered something completely different; the annual Scarecrow Festival was under way: get your map from the post office and hunt down the scarecrows that have been made by the families and businesses of the village. Keeping an eye out, along with all the other hunters, was a pleasant diversion. My favourite entry was the old married couple, still very much in love, sitting having a champagne and smoked salmon lunch outside the Earlsferry Care Home. It gave me hope for the future! My own rather less salubrious lunch was devoured at an empty beach just underneath Kincraig Hill. Afterwards, I followed the low path option and came to the famous chain walk. Meg and I negotiated our way along the coastline without using the first couple of chains, but working our way along the cliffs without falling into the sea became ever more difficult without holding onto the shiny links. For Meg's sake I retreated and took the high path over Kincraig Hill.

I continued round Largo Bay along the wide, sandy beach; with the tide out, I felt as though I was cutting corners off my journey. I passed through Largo, one-time home to Alexander Selkirk, the real-life Robinson Crusoe, and reached the seaside holiday town of Leven. After 5pm on a Bank Holiday Monday, the High Street at nearby Methil was eerily quiet, the only noise being the occasional banging of a pub door. Outside one of the pubs, a smoker bent down to pat Meg, missed her completely and toppled forwards onto the ground, his outstretched arms preventing any further damage. Not comfortable at all in this urban environment, I passed through Buckhaven and into East Wemyss, where I was too tired to pay much attention to the caves. I asked around for a place to camp and was directed to a grassy field, just off the Coastal Path, which was perfect.

The next morning, sea birds were diving off the old pier underneath Wemyss Castle. I stopped for coffee at a café by the harbour at Dysart, a mining town for 500 years until 1980; this historic village, its whitewashed houses sparkling in the morning sun, is overlooked by the fortified tower of Serf's Church, where cannons defended the occupants from marauding 16th-century English pirates.

Climbing up above the harbour, I strolled by the bluebells of Ravenscraig Wood and passed the ruins of 15th-century Ravenscraig Castle, started by James II, before entering Kirkcaldy, whose famous sons include the 12th-century wizard Michael Scott and the 18th-century father of economics, Adam Smith. A more recent graduate of the 'Lang Toon' is former PM Gordon Brown. Kirkcaldy is also the home of Raith Rovers FC. After one big win, the BBC infamously reported: 'They'll be dancing in the streets of Raith tonight'. Many years later, in a 1995 UEFA cup tie, Kirkcaldy folk were dancing in any street they could find after the Rovers went in at half time 1-0 up against Bayern Munich in Germany (although they eventually succumbed 2-1).

I admired the new leisure centre building, imagining the hot showers, but I couldn't linger. The entire esplanade was closed for renovations. Continuing south past the sparse remains of Seafield Tower, I followed the railway to Kinghorn where I got hijacked into buying coffee and a cake. As I walked past a little outdoor café, a fella stood up and said there was water for the dog. Meg saw the bowl and ran over for a drink. 'Are you staying for a coffee yourself?' he enquired. I could hardly say no as Meg guzzled away at the contents of the bowl. Anyway, I sat by the sandy beach and chatted to the other coffee drinkers, whilst admiring the salesmanship of my host.

On the cliffs between Kinghorn and Burntisland was where it all began! On a wild, stormy night, King Alexander III of Scotland fell from his horse and over the cliffs to his death. His desire to be with his new French Queen and to create a male heir to the throne led to his untimely death. The only recognised heir to the throne of Scotland was a three-year-old granddaughter, Margaret, who was a daughter to the King of Norway. As mentioned earlier, Margaret died on her journey to Scotland beginning a constitutional crisis.

A monument squeezed between the railway and the main road marks the spot where Alexander fell from his horse. An ancient plaque reads:

> Quen Alysandyr Oure King wes dede
> That Scotland led in luive and le
> Away wes sonce of ale and brede
> Of wyne and wax, of gamyn and gle
> our gold wes changed into lede
> Chryste! Borne into virgynyte
> Succour Scotland and Remede
> That stad is in perplexyte.

On the promenade at Burntisland, despite the weather being overcast, the benches were filled with people staring

The site where Alexander III fell to his death in 1286, sparking the Wars of Independence.

out quietly across the Forth, as if anxiously awaiting the return of fishermen after a storm. In 1633, King Charles I was returning to England after a coronation tour of Scotland when he lost his baggage in a ferry accident just off the coast here. The *Blessing of Burntisland* sank in a squall, taking with it the King's goods and some of his attendants – this priceless baggage awaits discovery.

I crossed the High Street and continued along to Aberdour. The 12th-century tower house at Aberdour was built upon and expanded by successive Earls of Morton. The visitor staff were friendly and the remains are impressive but I couldn't find any Bruce stories. A private road leads to Dalgety Bay, where there were warnings about radioactivity caused by luminous paint on instruments from World War II aircraft which were chucked into the bay by the MOD. I soldiered on.

Donibristle Bay opens out onto the Firth of Forth and has great views across to Leith as well as further west to the Forth Bridges. The bay is surrounded by private housing. I asked a local inhabitant if he knew anything of the battle that had taken place here in 1317. He didn't but what we do know is that an English force landed at the bay here and began looting and pillaging. The Sheriff of Fife was not eager to attack the strong contingent of pilferers. The Bishop of Dunkeld arrived on the scene with some reinforcements and shamed the Scots into attacking their enemies. This they did successfully, driving the English back into the Forth.

I camped near the old quarry outside Inverkeithing and in the morning I headed into the ancient town on my way to Dunfermline, passing a couple of reminders from the 14th century – the mercat cross and the gothic tower of the kirk from which Bruce issued two charters.

Dunfermline, an ancient and historic town, was the nation's capital in the 11th century during the reign of King Malcolm Canmore and his wife Margaret. They had six children and this royal line was only extinguished with Alexander III's untimely death. I approached the abbey with a little trepidation; here, I was catching up with Robert the Bruce at his final resting place. As I stepped inside, light streamed through the stained-glass windows above me. Straight ahead was the tomb of the hero king. I approached and although not a religious

Dunfermline Abbey, Bruce's final resting place.

person, I whispered a few words and solemnly paid my respects for a moment or two. The impressive tombstone lies under the pulpit stair of the church, which I find disrespectful.

Unbelievably, the King's remains were almost lost: during the Reformation, the abbey and the magnificent tomb built for the hero king were damaged; this part of the church, being altogether too ornate, was deemed unworthy for worship and was deserted by the flock. Eventually, the ceiling collapsed. Only in 1818, during the reconstruction of the kirk, was the King's body accidentally discovered inside a stone vault in the abbey floor, under where the high altar would have been situated. The body was wrapped in a cloth-of-gold shroud and covered in sheet lead. The skeleton was identified beyond doubt as Bruce because the chest cavity had been broken open. (Bruce's heart was removed upon his death.) By the time the body was re-interred, it wasn't quite as whole as it had been. A toe was missing – which found its way to Loch Awe – and two front teeth had been removed from the skull. A cast of the skull was taken and a copy of this cast is on display at the abbey. The large skull is quite terrifying and has some significant features, including damage to the left eye socket and cheek bone. The stained-glass windows of the abbey feature Bruce, Wallace, Moray and Douglas; if you look closely, you can see a spider. Another window features the Last Supper, with two of the disciples' faces changed to those of the benefactors of the abbey. Adjoining the abbey are the ruins of Dunfermline Palace which was begun by Robert the Bruce – his son David, was born here. The palace was further developed by later kings, but Charles I was the last monarch to begin life here as the royal residence fell into ruin when the Stuarts moved to London.

I wasn't quite ready to say my goodbyes to Bruce as yet. He was still alive and well in my mind and with a lot of unfinished business. I headed for Lothian, so often the decimated battleground of the Wars of Independence.

CHAPTER 9

Lothian

CROSSING THE FORTH Road Bridge, I noticed posters for the Samaritans reminding people that they were only a phone call away, but my thoughts were entirely positive as I crossed this iconic structure and looked out over the beautiful Forth Estuary and across to the macho railway bridge. After the first railway bridge over the Tay collapsed there was never going to be a repeat with this super-strong giant upon which construction began only three years later – at the time, it was the biggest cantilever bridge in the world. Sadly, almost as many people died in the construction of the Forth Rail Bridge as died in the Tay in 1879, when 75 lives were lost.

At South Queensferry, I started on an excellent route into the city of Edinburgh following a disused railway, but it was only a brief respite from the traffic. At the village of Dalmeny, I headed east and found the road to Cramond to be closed. I was diverted through the verdant and lamb-filled Dalmeny Estate. Walking along the estate roads through lush fields and mature woodland was peaceful and contemplative. I did try talking to the passing cyclists as they commuted home, but many seemed bemused by my friendliness and could only grunt in

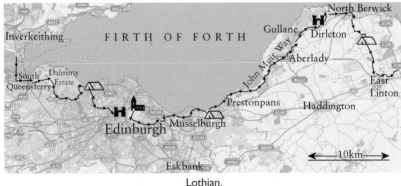

Lothian.

reply. The estate shepherd was much friendlier and when her curiosity was satisfied about the contents of Meg's bag, she told me that the estate belonged to the 7th Earl of Rosebery, whose grandfather was Prime Minister, briefly, at the end of the 19th century and whose grandmother was of the famous Rothschilds family and, in her day, one of the richest women in Britain. She returned to the 1,250 sheep over which she watched – hopefully the flock would be strengthened, albeit temporarily, by 1,800 newborn lambs before spring was out. I left the estate regretfully and crossed a 500-year-old bridge over the River Almond and walked through Cramond and prosperous Barnton, where the hedges were high and the gates electric. The thought of a warm shower kept me going as I headed to the Edinburgh Caravan Club campsite on the fringes of the city. It had been a long, exhausting day. My early start at the quarry at Inverkeithing seemed aeons ago. Despite the lateness of my arrival, I was warmly welcomed by the staff before I made my way to the green, which I had all to myself.

I spent my day of rest, minimising the time that my feet were connected to the ground. I read my book, made some notes, tried some Sudoku, ate, and ate some more. On day 54 I headed south, through the housing estates of Muirhouse and Drylaw, towards the city centre. The estates were much like many others and I didn't learn much, but as I neared the city centre, I did meet a lady who welcomed me to Edinburgh and gave me a bar of chocolate. At 85 years old she knew her city well; after I complimented her on her youthful appearance, Jean proceeded to tell me that for her birthday she had gotten a tattoo. A real extrovert, she asked me if I wanted to see it; I was terrified as to where it might be. However, she pulled up her sleeve to show me her bicep, upon which was engraved a top hat. Why a top hat? 'Well, in 1944, I worked at the Pally. My uniform was top hat and tails and I had to frisk all the American airmen going into the dancehall.' From her bag she pulled out a black and white picture of herself in younger days, resplendent in her uniform. 'I loved ma job,' she said, with a hint of wistfulness.

Following Queensferry Road, heading towards the New Town and just before Princes Street, I reached 'Randolph Cliff', a street from

The north crags below Edinburgh Castle were scaled by the Scots in 1314.

where you could view the volcanic crags which Thomas Randolph's forces scaled in 1314 to attack Edinburgh Castle. By January 1314, Bruce had recovered most of Scotland from his opponents. In terms of significant castles, only the royal fortresses of Stirling, Berwick, Roxburgh, Bothwell and Edinburgh remained in the hands of his enemies. Knowing that Edward II had made demands from across three kingdoms for forces to launch a massive reconquest of Scotland, Bruce ordered a redoubling of efforts to capture Edinburgh and Roxburgh castles and deny the English King any sanctuary within Lothian. Bruce's army had no major siege engines at this time, nor was there time to starve out the garrisons, so ingenuity, guile and determination would be the Scots' foremost weapons.

King Robert's chief lieutenant and the future Guardian of Scotland was charged with capturing Edinburgh Castle. It was an incredibly difficult proposition. Situated on the remnants of an ancient volcano, Edinburgh Castle was one of the foremost strengths within the kingdom. Fortuitously, William Francis, a local man whose father was part of the castle garrison, came forward. Living within the fortress, William was parted from his sweetheart in the town. Undaunted, the intrepid Romeo had figured out a route by which he could scale the seemingly impossible cliff so that he could visit his love and return to the castle without being missed. Seizing the opportunity, Randolph gathered together a small, lithe group and followed the young man up the rock-face to the foot of the stone walls, using specially devised ladders. A diversionary attack upon the main gate allowed them to scale the castle walls unnoticed. Attacking from within, Randolph's men won their way to the gate, opened it and let the main body of Scots charge in to overwhelm the castle garrison. In line with policy, Edinburgh Castle was destroyed.

The reducing of castles was of a much greater permanence than winning a battle. It made it difficult for an occupying force to return and 'lord it over' the local population and Bruce did not have to use precious resources and troops garrisoning castles. There would have been a huge morale swing as fortresses came crashing down: the Scots would have been delighted at the removal of grasping garrisons. To the English who built, strengthened and improved many castles, it would have sapped morale to see all their work in Scotland undone. To local populations, castles occupied by English soldiers would have been a sign not only of English military domination but also of the introduction more heavy-handed English justice and taxation. When the castle was gone so were the structures of English local government. This was another reason for the Scots resisting English occupation as they did, and possibly one that has been underplayed! The introduction of English taxation, which was higher than taxation imposed by Scottish monarchs, was never going to be a popular measure. And despite English Justice giving more liberty to people, it was also more severe, which may have weighed more heavily on people's minds. Also, English Justice was more centralised and reduced the power of Scots nobles. Holding the power of 'pit and gallows' gave them great power within their own territories.

I crossed Princes Street and heaved myself up The Mound, an artificial hill which connects the most famous street of the New Town, with the streets of the Old Town that lead to the Royal Mile. Meg had special permission to visit Edinburgh Castle, and as we waited for our specially appointed guides, she did her bit for the tourist trade by posing for Japanese tourists. Soon, Nigel and Emma from Historic

Scotland came down to greet us, and led us towards the gatehouse, where I came face to face once more with Bruce – his noble figure cast in bronze welcomed us to the fortress. Entering the castle, we wound our way uphill past hundreds of years of history to the summit of the volcanic remains upon which sat St Margaret's Chapel, a small, rectangular Norman church dedicated to the 11th-century Queen, who did much to establish the Roman Church in Scotland. The oldest remaining building within the castle, it survived, at least in part, Bruce's destruction, although the King did latterly provide money to have it repaired. Within the church, the chancel was separated from the nave by a decorative Norman arch, below which a kneeling pad invited me to make a short prayer before the altar of St Margaret. The quiet chapel was evocatively lit by five small, stained-glass windows that induced a feeling of peace and tranquillity, but not religious fervour.

Outside, amongst the hordes of visitors – some of the one million plus that visit each year – we dodged our way to David II's tower. Bruce's son rebuilt Edinburgh Castle and the remains of his 14th-century tower are hidden deep within the bowels of the current fortifications. Nigel took me down a wobbly metal staircase to show me the base of the ancient tower, which was enclosed completely in the 16th century by the construction of the Half Moon Battery. In the semi-dark, I clambered over the rough bedrock from which the ancient walling sprung; this was as close as I would get to replicating Randolph's feat. Ascending once more, we entered by the original 14th-century entrance. Below my feet was a pit, ready to drop unwanted visitors into a dark chasm. Nigel explained that a series of doors would have been required to be opened to enter the castle. If you didn't go through the correct door, you would step into the abyss.

What I was keen to see next was the Stone of Destiny. The queue snaked round the Royal Palace but I was allowed to sneak in by a side entrance to visit the Crown Room where the Scottish Crown Jewels and the stone were on display. In the centre of a small dark room, within a brightly lit glass case, were the precious artefacts of the Stuart Royalty and a block of Perthshire sandstone, masquerading as the Stone of Destiny.

The Stone of Destiny was the legendary seat upon which ancient Scottish monarchs were crowned. It has the most amazing origin myth, created to enhance the ancient lineage of the Scottish monarchy. This exuberant tale relates that the stone was Jacob's pillow in the wild, upon which, according to the Bible, he dreamed of a ladder to heaven. Eventually, according to the legend, it was brought to Ireland by the prophet, Jeremiah. The Scots then brought the stone from their kingdom in Ireland to their kingdom in Argyll, where it was used as a seat upon which their kings were crowned. From there it was brought to Scone when the Scots took over the Pictish kingdom.

In 1296, after attempting to abolish the Scottish monarchy, Edward I made a beeline for Scone Abbey, stole the stone and sent it to Westminster Abbey. Thereafter, English, then latterly British monarchs have sat upon the stone during their coronation ceremony.

The stone within the case was oblong and weighed 152kg. Unadorned, apart from a small cross in one corner, it was quarried in Perthshire, close to Scone Abbey. Thus the stone in front of me was of Pictish origin and having seen the wonderful Pictish sculpture on Sueno's Stone, the Maiden Stone and the St Andrews Sarcophagus it seemed incredible that Pictish, then Scottish monarchs, were crowned upon such a rough, unfinished and unadorned piece of stone.

Statue of Bruce at St Giles Kirk.

Saying goodbye to Emma and Nigel, I walked back down the Royal Mile. This street held particularly good memories for me; I remember floating downhill towards Waverley Station after a meeting with Luath Press when they took a chance on an untried writer and agreed to publish a book on my proposed walk to follow in Bonnie Prince Charlie's footsteps.

I stopped at St Giles Cathedral, the High Kirk of Edinburgh; I was looking for another statue of Robert the Bruce. After looking both outside and inside, I failed to see him. I asked a guide, 'Could you tell me where the statue of Robert the Bruce is?' Quick as a flash, she retorted 'Stirling'. I stood, unmoving. When the lady saw the grim look on my face, she called over another guide who confirmed there was no statue of Robert the Bruce inside or outside the building. Livid at being made out to be stupid, I wasn't sure enough of my facts to put up much resistance. I walked off and continued to look around the church, too annoyed to take in any details. Outside the 14th-century kirk, above the main entrance door, there were a number of statues, and as I exited the church the second guide was looking up at them. Together but very much apart, we both stared up and eventually agreed upon one of the statues of being 'Good King Robert'. The crowned figure, battleaxe in hand (it wasn't rocket science, was it!), looked down sternly upon us. Appeased by this belated success, I continued on.

At the foot of the Royal Mile, the ruins of Holyrood Abbey stand alongside the Palace of Holyrood. My friend Tessa was waiting for me and she brought treats for Meg and spoiled me with lunch at the palace cafe. Outside, I met up with George, a freelance reporter, and Colin, a photographer. Historic Scotland were expecting a canine visitor and as we approached the Iron Gates, Kirsty greeted our arrival. The royal corgis couldn't hold a candle to Meg, who entered Holyrood Abbey accompanied by a guide, a poet, a journalist, a photographer and me, the lowly lead holder.

One of the most impressive of Scotland's religious houses, Holyrood Abbey suffered significant damage from the usual suspects – English soldiers and the Reformation. The ruins are now overshadowed by the adjoining 16th-century royal palace, but a vision of its greatness remains. The walls of the nave still stand, but only the foundations remain of the more decorated and grand part of the church, the choir. In 1322, Edward II burned the church when he brought an army of over 20,000 men to Scotland. Bruce retired in front of this huge force, enforcing a scorched earth policy on Lothian. All crops were spoiled and cattle driven off to deny the invading army any provisions. When the King of England's supply fleet was scattered by both Flemish privateers and bad weather, the starving army returned across the border, having achieved nothing. Bruce followed up this incursion with his own invasion of England, where he defeated an English army at the Battle of Old Byland, and almost captured Edward and his Queen at Rievaulx Abbey in North Yorkshire.

Having revelled in our VIP treatment, Meg and I followed Tessa into the green hills of Holyrood Park, on a path alongside Hunter's Bog – a route frequented by both Mary Queen of Scots and Bonnie Prince Charlie. Our shortcut south soon had us descending alongside Arthur's Seat as we headed for the 'Innocent Railway' – a tunnel in the residential St Leonards area, the entrance to which would have been impossible to find without assistance. Taking its name from either its safety record or its slow rate of travel, the Innocent Railway brought coal and an ever-increasing number of passengers from Dalkeith in the east of the city to Saint Leonard's in the city centre. The 517m tunnel under Holyrood Park was built in 1831 and is one of the earliest surviving railway tunnels in the UK. It became a walking route in 1981, part of National Cycle Route 1 in 1994 and in 2014 it became part of the extended John Muir Way, which now runs from Helensburgh on the west coast to John Muir's birthplace at Dunbar. I thanked Tessa for her company, her guidance and of course lunch and headed into the downward-sloping tunnel. Well lit, the quiet tunnel allowed uninterrupted progress and I popped out near to Duddingston Loch. At Brunstane, somehow I failed to read the plentiful signs properly and ended up following the road through Joppa, rather than by continuing along the Brunstane Burn to Fisherrow. If followed properly, this route is an excellent, safe way for walkers and cyclists to enter or exit Edinburgh. At neat little Fisherrow harbour, the fishing fleet has been replaced by pleasure boats, but I didn't dilly dally here, I was hoping to make it to the campsite at Levenhall before it closed for the evening. I left the promenade to take a shortcut along New Street, crossed the River Esk and hurried along past the man-made lagoons of Levenhall Links.

'Campsite' turned out to be misnomer. Dummohr Holiday Park offered caravans, bothies, plain lodges, Octo Lodges or Hexi Lodges, to dissuade weary hikers from their tent. However, on a sunny evening I was perfectly happy with my canvas companion – my expectations of comfort having slipped so much that toilets, showers and a level pitch, gave me enough of a thrill.

At eight o'clock the next morning, I was packing up my gear outside the toilet block when a small, four-wheel drive vehicle belonging to the campsite pulled up. My friend Iain, who I had been expecting, jumped out, sporting a cheery grin and a daysack. My companion for the day was full of enthusiasm and support and it was uplifting to be with company. Iain knew the area well and we blethered away.

Continuing alongside the Firth of Forth, we passed through the village of Prestonpans, scene of a Jacobite victory in 1746, the memory of which is kept alive by a very active charitable trust. In 2010, the trust commissioned a 104m tapestry telling the story of Bonnie Prince Charlie, from his landing in Scotland in April 1745 to his departure for England eight months later at the head of a Jacobite army. The longest tapestry in the world, it was sewn in the main by volunteers from East Lothian with each of the 104 panels taking on average 300 hours to produce. It has since toured Scotland, impressing and educating in equal measure.

Iain and I were talking about football, camping and the real world, in fact, anything but history, until we got to the ancient town of Aberlady. Resting on a bench by the 18th-century mercat cross and without being asked, I mentioned how the historical novels of Nigel Tranter had introduced me (along with countless others) to Scottish history. They had kept me immersed for a number of years as I read of people and events, from Columba to the Jacobites. I remember vividly the horror of my first foray into Nigel Tranter's novels: the *Bruce* trilogy opens with Edward I humiliating John Balliol in Stracathro Church, stripping him of his crown, his kingdom and his emblazoned coat. Tranter used to write as he walked along the coastline here, making shorthand notes, and taking inspiration from his surroundings. He lived until the grand old age of 90 and was a lovely man whom I had

A memorial to Nigel Tranter at Aberlady Bay.

the pleasure of meeting. I felt a sharp tug of emotion when, quite by accident, we came across a memorial to him at Aberlady Bay.

...he was always glad to return here, to... the unending sigh of the waves on the far sandbar at the mouth of the bay, the calling of the sea-birds, the quacking of mallard and the honking of the wavering wild geese skeins which crisscrossed the sky.

from *Crusader* by Nigel Tranter

As we walked along the roadside towards Gullane, a jeep whizzed by, the driver exclaiming a large 'O' as he passed. It looked awfully like my brother-in-law, Scott. Nicola had telephoned me first thing that morning to tell me that her mum had been taken to hospital overnight and to be ready to come home if her condition deteriorated any further. Talking to Iain during the morning we had discussed my predicament. Should I go home or keep walking? When the jeep's brake lights glowed and it turned around to come back towards us, I feared the worst. However, Scott's reaction when he pulled up was more of surprise rather than concern. By some outlandish fluke, he happened to be dropping off Lisa, my sister-in-law, at a hen party at nearby Archerfield, rather than being out searching for me. He updated me on his mum's condition, which he understated in typical male fashion, before I returned to my escapade and he returned to the real world.

Talking our way through Gullane, Iain and I ate our rations in the grounds of Dirleton Castle. The remains of the powerful, 13th-century castle are beautiful. Others thought the same, as we wandered round, we could hear a minister reciting wedding vows, deep down in the vaults underneath the Great Hall. Dirleton Castle is a tale of three families, who all contributed to the fortress over a period of 300 years. The Anglo-Norman family De Vaux built the first stone castle in the late 13th century, which was captured by the English in 1298 after a prolonged siege. Bruce's forces recaptured the castle sometime before 1314 and slighted it. Before its destruction, the castle consisted of three large circular towers and two square towers connected by a high curtain wall which enclosed the rocky outcrop on which the fortress stood. The main circular tower, the donjon, and one square tower survive from this period, but the other towers are gone and the other remains are later additions built by the Haliburtons in the 14th century and by the Ruthvens 200 years after that.

We continued on to the seaside resort of North Berwick, the 'Biarritz of the North'. As we walked into town, the entrance bells were clanging rhythmically in the bustling little shops of the Main Street. For over 1,000 years, tourists have been shopping at the town; in the first instance it was pilgrims, prior to heading for the harbour and making the oft-times dicey sailing across the Forth Estuary, on their way to the religious shrine at St Andrews. In 1413, 15,000 pilgrims made the journey to Fife and as a memento of their travel, they bought a badge confirming that they had undertaken the crossing. Iain took a train back to his car, which was parked at Wallyford Station. I continued on, and despite having Meg to talk to, the quiet was a little disheartening.

Passing through parkland at North Berwick Lodge, I headed towards and then around Berwick Law: rising up steeply, this ancient volcanic plug is famously topped by a whale jawbone, although with the last authentic bone collapsing in 2005, the current jawbone is a fibreglass replica donated by a mysterious benefactor. I crossed fields and followed an old track, the Leuchie Road, before camping within a patch of thick forest not far from the main trail. It was May and I still hadn't seen a midge the whole trip. My main motivation for setting off in mid-March had been to be avoid plagues of summer midges at the back end of the journey.

On a bright morning I followed farm tracks and crossed more fields to arrive on the outskirts of East Linton, where I followed the River Tyne. For a time, I walked with a local resident, our dogs sparking a conversation. Originally from south of the border, my riverside companion had been in East Linton for 20 years and although she liked it here, and the local community had been very welcoming, her part of England was still home. Travelling round the country with her job, she had encountered a fair amount of anti-English feeling. I didn't want to blame Edward I for this, we have had 700 years to get over it!

Following Bruce's success in the north and the west, Lothian was another massive challenge for the King. He was hampered by the fact that the major landholder and most important noble in Lothian, the Earl of Dunbar and March, took Edward I as his liege lord in 1296 and when the son took over the earldom in 1308 he remained loyal to the Plantagenets. Bruce put smaller landowners still loyal to Edward II under increasing pressure after 1309. Their lands and people were harassed, although by the payment of cash, truces could be secured.

The English position in Lothian was strengthened by their control of a number of top notch castles including Edinburgh, Berwick, Roxburgh and Selkirk as well as a number of lesser but still impressive strongholds such as Dirleton and Dunbar. There were good communications between these castles and the majority of them were within a short distance of the North Sea coast, which English naval power still dominated. There was no quick method of victory in Lothian, only a war of continual attrition against the strongholds and landowners.

Lothian's position was further complicated by the fact that it lay on the campaign trail, and was harassed by both English and Scots.

Invading armies could be expected to requisition food stocks and lay lands to waste whose owners supported the opposing cause. Defending Scottish armies would operate a scorched earth policy, to prevent the enemy finding any supplies. Imagine being cleared off your farm, your crops burned, your livestock slaughtered and the meat spoiled by your own supposed king! I know which side I'd have chosen. Robert the Bruce, either stick up for us or feck off. These guerrilla tactics Bruce employed must have required a high degree of single-mindedness on the part of the King, knowing the hardship he was causing, but they were effective. In 1322, the only food that an invading English army found during its journey north was a single cow. Referring to the cost of the ineffective expedition, an English general remarked it was the dearest cow in history.

I reached Buist's embankment which protected the surrounding reclaimed farmland from flooding by the tidal estuary. The tide was out as I walked along the dyke looking out over exposed mudflats to Sandy Hirst, a long wood covered spit of land. I was within the John Muir country park and I stopped to chat to a couple of ladies, one of whom had just returned from a walking tour of the monasteries in the Himalayas. Here was me on such a crazy and wild adventure that my brother-in-law drove past me in his car!

Passing the lounging llamas and the narrow gauge railway of East Links Family Park, a place I knew well from when my kids were younger, I raced against the tide to take a shortcut across the southern part of Belhaven Bay, but I was defeated before I could reach the rather isolated footbridge that crosses the Biel Water. Still muttering and cursing about how domestic my adventure was, I was forced to retrace my steps and walk around the bay to Dunbar.

Two battles which led to the subjugation of Scotland were fought at Dunbar. John Balliol was defeated by Edward 1 in 1296, and in 1651 a large Scots army was defeated by Oliver Cromwell's Roundhead army, paving the way for the occupation of the country 1651–60. The town was also the childhood home of John Muir, the great naturalist, father of the American National Parks and an early environmentalist. He enthused about the outdoors and said 'of all the paths you take in life,

A tooth-like fragment of Dunbar Castle.

make sure a few of them are dirt.'

The main seat of the Earl of Dunbar and March was, quite naturally, Dunbar Castle. The scant remains of this great fortress, which once controlled the entrance to the harbour as well as a vast Earldom, are now crumbling into the sea. Probably because it was virtually impregnable, Bruce ignored this castle. For a while he probably wished he hadn't, because it was the Earl of Dunbar's letter to Edward II that spurred the English King to invade Scotland in 1314. The castle survived until the 16th century when it was slighted on the orders of the Scottish parliament. Its destruction was completed by Robert William Thomson, who invented a technique for electrically firing explosive charges. Equally interesting was an information board telling the story of Robert Wilson, a local lad and prolific inventor, who demonstrated the first practical ship's propeller in 1827.

Still following the coast southwards on an extension of the John Muir Way which runs from Dunbar to Cockburnspath, I left town on a concrete embankment between the beach and the golf course. From Barnes Ness lighthouse, large sand dunes gave some shelter from the stiff breeze as I approached Torness nuclear power station. Massive concrete defences protect this facility from the ravages of the sea. Patrolling behind the parapet of the outer wall, the wind pulling at my hair, I searched the distant horizon for imminent attack, feeling secure in the strength of the fortification. The inner walls with narrow slits were like gigantic versions of the pillboxes built to defend the Normandy coast from Allied attack. After Thorntonloch Caravan Park, the path climbed uphill to follow the high clifftop, where crop filled fields pushed right up to the cliff edge. At a break in the cliffs I descended into a ravine to meet the Bilsdean Burn as it tumbled down to a stony beach before I clocked what could have been an easily missed sign that put me on a steeply climbing path once again. From Dumglass I made my way onwards to the ancient village of Cockburnspath, where at the village hall I was able to get some desperately needed fresh water. The 500-year-old mercat cross celebrated the marriage of James IV and Margaret Tudor, which led ultimately and peacefully to the Union of the Scottish and English Crowns. Cockburnspath is the start of both the Southern Upland Way (340km coast to coast, finishing at Port Patrick in the southwest) and the Berwickshire Coastal Path, which terminates at Berwick-Upon-Tweed, my destination. Almost stumbling from exhaustion at this point, I rejoined the coastline at Pease Bay, where the clifftop path, frustratingly, descends once again – this time to a caravan park. Beyond the resort, a wooden staircase ascended the cliffs one final time. I collapsed in a heap in a field, beside the ancient Norman church of St Helens at Aldcambus. Little remains of the small, sandstone kirk and the grave markers were lying as though

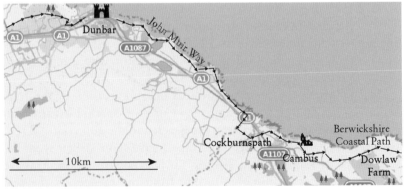

Dunbar to Dowlaw Farm.

The Berwickshire Coastal Path.

Squeezed between the railway and the cliffs as Meg and I get closer to Berwick.

the dead had risen up and escaped their earthly prison, but it gave me a link to the past.

In a wood at Aldcambus, Bruce was preparing engines for the siege of Berwick (1317) when a monk brought him the papal truce, addressed to 'Robert, Governor of Scotland'.

'I listen to no bulls till I am treated as king, and have made myself master of Berwick,' was the haughty reply; but the monk was later robbed of the unopened missive, which doubtless found its way into Bruce's hands.[29]

For his refusal to open the Pope's letter and obey the terms of a proposed truce with England, Bruce was excommunicated. The King was cut off from the Church, and forbidden from participating in religious ceremonies. At a time of universal religious belief this was a massive blow. Should he die, he would be unable to ascend to heaven and would be consigned to eternal purgatory, or worse!

After a good night's sleep (as they almost all were) I continued on the coastal path, passing Siccar point where in 1788, James Hutton, the self-taught founder of modern Geology, observed the layers of Greywacke rock that over millennia had tilted vertically before being overlaid with

Looking back the way I have come on the Berwickshire Coastal Path.

layers of Red Sandstone. This formation, known as an unconformity provided the final proof to back up his theory that the Earth is millions of years old, rather than 6,000 years as given in the Bible.

The path headed inland for a time. At Redhaugh Farm, the farmer emerged from a barn and asked me to put Meg on a lead. He also advised me to let go of said lead if the large herd of cattle in the field through which the path passed decided to charge at us. No way was I walking through that field! Once up on the hillside I kept to the adjoining one, where a broken-down, drystane dyke kept Meg hidden from the 40 or so beasts.

Soon I was once again following the weaving path that crowns the high cliffs, the land's rugged edge far below drawn by the white line of breaking waves. Before the final pull to St Abb's Head, a national nature reserve, I looked back and let out an involuntary 'Wow!' at the stunning view: the line of stony-faced headlands protruding into the sea, looking like a herd of submerging elephants.

After feeding on some sticky figs, the resulting sugar rush sent me singing up a tarmac road towards the peak of the promontory and the St Abb's Head Lighthouse. From this high perch I could look down upon the vertical rock faces where the clamouring cries of the nesting seabirds fought amongst the whooping wind to be heard. Powering on round Starney Bay, I descended to St Abb's where I had one of the most enjoyable stops of the entire trip. It was a Monday and I almost had the tiny, picturesque village to myself as I sat at a perfectly placed picnic bench overlooking the harbour. Under the blazing sun, Meg lay crashed out amongst the daisies while I relaxed with my lunch, watching small boats come and go and a mariner preparing his sailing dinghy. Things in short supply are often held in high regard and I savoured every minute of my break from walking.

At Coldingham Bay the waves rolled up onto the golden sands, lapping over my worn-out shoes. A line of brightly painted beach huts edged the beach. I half expected the 'put upon' husband of British seaside holiday postcards to emerge, tubby and sunburned, with a stripey all-over swimsuit and a knotted handkerchief covering a bald head.

The busy harbour at Eyemouth dates back to the 13th century – after the loss of Berwick-upon-Tweed, Eyemouth became the Scottish port closest to the continent and in the 18th and 19th centuries was a notorious haven for smuggling. The most infamous moment in the town's history is the Eyemouth Disaster of 1881, when 189 fishermen, two-thirds of them from Eyemouth, died in a great storm that struck southern Scotland.

Walking along the shore by the golf course, I left the town, chatting as I went to Martin and June from Prestonpans. The route soon became a clifftop walk once more as I edged towards Burnmouth. Lower Burnmouth nestles at the foot of the cliffs but I didn't have the energy to drop down and climb back up again. I asked advice from a local man, out spraying sticky willows with a small bottle of weedkiller to prevent his dogs getting covered – surely a case of fingers in a dyke. He advised me of a route where I could remain on the clifftops and I emerged onto the A1 at virtually the last village in Scotland, Burnmouth (upper), and followed the road briefly before cutting off onto an old track which ran under the railway and led me back to the coastal path once again. Squeezed between the railway

Looking up to the remains of Berwick Castle.

and the cliffs, I cleared away sheep crap and nettles to camp on a hummock high above the shore.

The next day I continued towards the walled town of Berwick-upon-Tweed with thoughts of 14th-century English aggression starting to agitate me. If there was any wrestling over shopping trolleys in the aisles of Lidl, I'd be ready. So much for my 700 years to get over it! England's most northerly town, Berwick, belonged to Scotland until 1482, when it was taken from James III by the Duke of Gloucester, the future Richard III. At one time Scotland's richest seaport, it was made an example of by the English at the outset of the Wars of Independence. In 1296, Edward I captured the town and castle and slaughtered the townspeople – 7,500 men, women and children, according to one chronicler. Edward then set about re-establishing Berwick as an English town. After defeating the Scottish Army at Dunbar, Scottish resistance to the English King collapsed and Edward stripped John Balliol of his Scottish crown. Scots nobles, landowners, and men of a certain standing swore fealty to the English King (calling himself Lord Paramount of Scotland) for their lands. This was often done in person, although some of these expressions of fealty were collected by Edward's administrators. In all, what the English King called his Ragman's Roll contained over 1,500 names. The word 'rigmarole', my grannie's favourite word, derives from this event. Robert Bruce himself was one who gave his fealty to Edward at Berwick Castle. In 1306 the Countess of Buchan was kept in a wooden cage, hung from the same castle, as a punishment for placing the crown upon Bruce's head during his coronation at Scone a few months earlier.

Both Edward I and Edward II used Berwick as a springboard from which to launch invasions into Scotland. As Bruce recovered his kingdom, Berwick was denied him, even after victory at Bannockburn. The Scots made many attempts to win the walled town and mighty castle back, including in 1312 when, during a night attack, a barking dog gave the game away. In 1316, the Scots were at the town's walls again and were once more repulsed. Not until 1318 did they meet with more success. Word was brought that a Burgess of Berwick, Peter of Spalding, would allow the Scots into the town via the section of wall which he oversaw. A force led by Thomas Randolph and Sir James Douglas successfully stormed the town, and besieged the castle – 11 weeks later the starving garrison submitted. Bruce made special efforts to restore the town to its previous prominence by repairing the castle, heightening the city walls and granting charters and rights. Scottish families were given financial inducements to settle in the town, but it never sustained the re-emergence that Bruce envisaged and while it was in Scots' hands the English continually attacked. When town walls were rebuilt in the Elizabethan period, they enclosed a town of only half the size that the previous walls had enclosed. By today's standards Berwick is a small town, with a population of around 12,000. The people retain something of a dual identity: in 2008, when ITV conducted an unofficial referendum, 60 per cent of Berwickers responded that they would prefer to rejoin Scotland.

Above the mighty River Tweed there remain only a few particles of the mighty fortress that was Berwick Castle. The remains of the keep exist on the cliffs above the river, and the remains of a 13th-century curtain wall, known as the White Wall, run steeply down to the river.

Norham Castle, an English strength which Bruce was determined to capture.

Regrettably to non-anoraks, most of the castle was dismantled with the building of the railway station. Despite the loss of Berwick and the removal of the last remaining English garrison from Scotland, Edward II was not yet ready to give up on Scotland and in 1319 his army of 8,000 besieged Berwick. The town and castle were successfully held by Walter Steward, the progenitor of the Stewart Kings.

Even before Bannockburn, Bruce had been changing the nature of the war by making bold attacks into England. Great raids were made into northern England by Bruce and his lieutenants. The objective was primarily to force Edward II to make peace with Scotland, and accept her as an independent neighbour. Of course the coin, cattle and corn collected helped to sustain and finance Bruce's war efforts. Towns such as Hexham, Durham and Lancaster were offered the choice of paying protection money, or being burned to the ground. As the years passed, the raids grew bolder and bolder, penetrating further and further south. Success bred success and the Scots completely dominated the north of England: Robert Bruce, Sir James Douglas, Thomas Randolph, Edward Bruce and Walter Steward became masters at leading fast-moving raiding armies. Cumbria and Northumbria were paralysed by fear and the Scots rampaged. To the English Treasury, northern

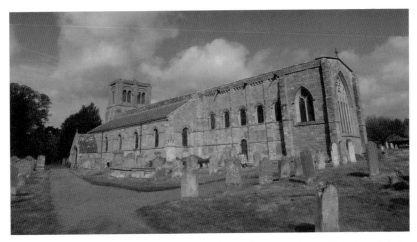

St Cuthbert's Church, Bruce's headquarters during the many sieges of Norham Castle.

England became a lost cause between 1314 and 1329 as taxation money was spent on buying off the Scots.

I headed for Norham, home of a spectacular castle which was a resolute defender of the English border where some key events in the Wars of Independence took place. I followed the A698 out of Berwick and when the pavement came to an end, I cut off on a back road towards Horncliffe, a sleepy little village situated within a bend of the mighty Tweed. So sleepy that the pub was shut. My plan for a pub lunch while a gathering storm passed was ruined. I walked down to the River Tweed and the storm rolled in. With thunder and lightning overhead, I abandoned my attempt to walk over Green Hill and decided to follow the winding river round to Norham. Soon, the rain subsided and the storm seemed to have passed, so I left the overgrown riverside path to start up the hill once again. When the sky cracked, banged and flashed once more, I scarpered back to the riverside, caution being the better part of valour. The weather gradually improved, as did the path; ducks and swans sailed up and down the peaceful river, whilst deer grazed nearby. As I entered a wooded area, a sign warned about the narrow, overgrown track. Thereafter, it was a rollercoaster ride on the ups and downs of the mucky path, my worn-out shoes providing zero traction. Funny how an adventure can be had with the simplest of things. Eventually the odds beat me and I slipped and fell, my rucksack pushing me down into a faceful of nettles, my eight-week-old beard at least saving me from a few stings. I soon lost all notion of where to leave the path to climb up to Norham Castle. Desperate to escape the slippery riverside, I followed a path by a small burn, hoping that the castle might be above me. When the path turned in the wrong direction, I scrambled up a smooth, bare bank, grabbing branches to pull myself up, and found myself in a field not too far from my destination.

The spectacular fortress was for 500 years a solid guardian of England's territory, built in a strong position overlooking a ford of the Tweed. Three walls of the five-storey tower remain, as well as the foundations of other buildings, including the great hall where King John Balliol gave homage to Edward I in 1292. Robert the Bruce besieged the castle on several occasions. The strong outer walls and the protection of the river on one side and a moat on the other aided the defenders. In early 1327, on the day that Edward III was crowned King of England, Bruce again failed to capture Norham Castle. Later that year, the Scots invaded England in strength and the boy King Edward marched with his army to confront a force led by Sir James Douglas and Thomas Randolph. The Scots humiliated the English King, using their knowledge of the territory, their mobile force and the element of surprise to outwit and evade the young King's army, and in one daring night attack Sir James almost captured him. In the end, the English failed to bring the Scots to battle and Bruce had shown that he could invade with impunity. In August 1327, he once more set siege to Norham Castle, as part of a general invasion of northern England. He began issuing charters of land in Northumbria to his supporters. The English government panicked, believing that Bruce was intent on annexing the region, and sent envoys to Berwick to begin peace negotiations.

Within the great tower, I took shelter from another spell of heavy rain. Meg took possession of the castle and barked wildly at some dusk-time visitors, her warnings echoing round the high walls. I camped, hidden away as usual, in nearby woodland. The following morning,

I walked through the village of Norham. St Cuthbert's Church dates from Norman times and was used as a headquarters by Bruce whilst his army besieged the castle. An early morning service of some sorts was going on within, so I didn't venture inside.

I headed back towards the Tweed, where the first bridge connecting Norham and Scotland was built in the 19th century, after a local doctor was drowned at the ford. For hundreds of years previously, the enmity caused in part by the ambitions of Edward I meant that a bridge of 100km in length wouldn't have spanned the gap between the river banks.

CHAPTER 10

Homeward Bound

IT WAS ANOTHER beautiful and bright morning as I settled into a day of back roads, once more in Scotland and heading for home via the country's 12th-century capital and the magnificent Border abbeys. I passed through the village of Birgham, where a treaty was signed between the Scots and English in 1286 shortly before the Maid of Norway died. The traffic was fairly busy after the village. When a funeral director waved me off the road I took the hint and continued along farm tracks to the outskirts of Kelso, passing the National Hunt Racecourse as I entered town.

Kelso Abbey was the largest of the Border abbeys, built to a twin tower and double cross design that is unique within Scotland. Only the ruins of the mighty west tower remain, the abbey having been systematically dismantled in the 16th century. Nearby, on a peninsula of land enclosed by the rivers Tweed and Teviot, was situated the medieval town of Roxburgh. I crossed the Tweed to reach this once thriving royal burgh which traded with France, Italy, the Netherlands and the Baltic

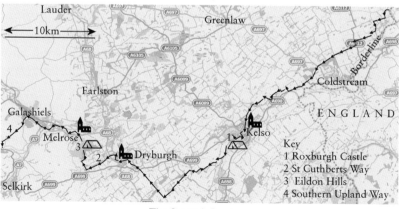

The Scottish Borders.

On a hilltop which once held a mighty fortress, looking over to Floors Castle, home of the Duke of Roxburghe.

states. Goods were transported down the Tweed to Berwick where they were exported to these foreign markets. The town was protected by a strong castle built in the 12th century by King David I, who won control of Northumbria as well as Scotland, and Roxburgh was at the centre of this expanded kingdom. However, future Scottish Kings were unable to hold onto gains made by David and eventually Roxburgh became a town on the unruly border, and suffered accordingly. When Berwick was lost to England permanently in 1482, Roxburgh lost its outlet to foreign markets and the town died. The memory of this busy burgh is kept alive (only just), in the names of the undulating green fields under which the remains of houses, churches, schools and royal mints lie: Vigorous Haugh is named after a burgess of the town; Friar's Haugh recalls the monks of a medieval friary.

I headed down to a path alongside the River Teviot and was eating my usual evening fare when a fisherman approached. He had seen the steam from my pot and feared I was about to camp by the bank, but when I assuaged his fears he told me a little of his catch history: in a fishing career spanning 50 years, Peter had caught 42 fish weighing over 20 pounds on the rivers Tweed and Teviot. Just downstream he had caught a fish of over 30 pounds which had taken over 40 minutes to land in the shallow water. The nearby Junction Pool, formed where the Tweed and Teviot meet, is world famous and the holy grail of salmon fishing in Scotland. With my mouth watering at the thought of all this tasty fish, I returned to my dried pasta and instant semolina.

Upon the tree-covered hillock between the rivers sit a few isolated fragments of stonework, the remains of Roxburgh Castle. Using my sticks to good effect I cleared a space amongst the nettles which had taken over the site and camped. From my tent flap I looked over to the splendid and sprawling Floors Castle, home of the Duke of Roxburghe. Was I jealous? Not one jot, freedom is a wonderful thing!

Roxburgh Castle lasted for 300 years until it was pulled down in 1460 by Scots sick of it being captured by the 'auld enemy' and used against them. It was held by the English in 1314 when James Douglas led a force of 60 men in an attempt to capture the castle. Dressed in black cloaks to hide their armour, they approached on hands and knees; the sentries, thinking they were a herd of cattle, took no notice! Rope ladders and grappling hooks got the Scots onto the

A suspension bridge over the River Tweed, with the Eildon Hills in the background.

battlements and they won the ensuing battle. Edward Bruce came to destroy Roxburgh Castle just as Robert Bruce oversaw the destruction of Edinburgh Castle. Quite possibly this was a symbolic gesture – only the royal family could be seen to destroy royal premises, or possibly the Bruce brothers had the most experience in undermining castle walls. Anyway, no Roxburgh ghosts put in an appearance overnight, despite the hundreds of people who must have died on this ground over the centuries. This includes the Scottish King, James II, who died nearby whilst besieging the castle – one of his cannons exploded and blew off his leg.

I was wakened at first light by Meg's trampling paws. Deer braying some distance away had startled her. She obviously felt brave enough to answer back this time, given the distances involved. With her barking still reverberating round my head, I decided on an early start and followed the green banks of the Teviot to the new village of Roxburgh, then continued west towards the Eildon Hills. A husband and wife drove past a couple of times before venturing to stop and ask if this was Meg. We had been spotted from their kitchen window and as they had read about our first adventure, they were curious as to what we were doing this time. Yet again, Meg was the one who had found fame but it was nice that people were pleased to see us in their own back yard.

The old church in the village of Maxton was given by the Bishop of Glasgow to the monks of Melrose in part compensation for the burning of their abbey in 1322. Here I stepped onto the St Cuthbert's Way, a 100km waymarked route between Melrose and Holy Island, which lies off the Northumberland coast. Walking through some woodland amongst ancient beech trees brought me down to the Tweed again and once more I followed the river for a while. Taking a shortcut onto some quiet country roads, I found myself herding hare and grouse towards St Boswells. Feeling slightly out of place in the village bookshop/café, I scoffed down tomato and beetroot soup, the tastiest and freshest fare that I had consumed in weeks.

Back by the Tweed, I headed over a suspension bridge to Dryburgh Abbey – another of the four great Border abbeys, where a decent set

Bruce's heart lies at Melrose Abbey.

of ruins remains. The mature parkland and the respectful quiet of the midweek visitors added to the feeling of peace and reverence. Edward II burned this abbey during his fruitless expedition of 1322, but the monks continued their ministry until the 16th century. A forward-thinking Earl of Buchan preserved the ruins in the 18th century, and within the church ruins is Sir Walter Scott's tomb.

On the St Cuthbert's Way once again, I was led towards a group of three small hills, prominent in an otherwise flat landscape – the Eildon Hills. These hills, or more accurately, this three-topped hill, once housed a significant Bronze Age population. At the foot of the hill, the Romans built a huge fort, Trimontium. Surrounded by woodland, these grass-topped eminences made a lovely spot to spend the last hour of the day and at 400m weren't too much of a climb. I surveyed the surrounding plains from the north top, once the site of a local tribe's hilltop fort, and then a Roman signalling tower.

After a windy night on the summit I set off early, charging downhill towards Melrose for my final meeting with the scattered remains of

Robert the Bruce. The ladies from the visitor centre let me in early and I had Melrose Abbey all to myself. In early morning sunshine, I strode purposefully towards what would have been the chapter house where Bruce's heart was buried. Meg, ahead of me as usual, spotted the small sandstone marker before I did. She made straight for it, paused and sniffed before rolling onto her back for a good scratch.

Here was the epilogue to the King's life.

In 1329, Robert the Bruce died of natural causes at his manor house near Dumbarton. His heart removed from his body and placed in a casket. The King had been unable to fulfil his desire to join a crusade to the Holy Land as atonement for his sins, but his heart was to be taken on crusade by Sir James Douglas, Scotland's greatest warrior. Douglas got no further than southern Spain where he was killed fighting a Moorish army at the Battle of Teba. His boiled bones were returned to Scotland and buried at St Bride's Kirk and the casket containing Bruce's heart was buried at Melrose Abbey. A casket – possibly, but not conclusively *the* casket – was uncovered in 1921, placed in a lead container and reburied. In 1996, it was dug up once more and reburied in 1998 in a ceremony attended by the leading politicians and dignitaries of the day. The spot is marked by a circular plaque depicting a saltire and a heart entwined, accompanied by a line from Barbour's *Bruce*: 'A noble hart may have nane ease. Gif freedom failye.'[30]

Bruce had been prepared to sacrifice everything, including what he believed was his place in heaven, in order to win Scotland back her freedom. What a fitting ending to his life, and almost to my own journey. From here on in I would be heading towards my own finale at Bannockburn, the scene of Bruce's greatest triumph.

I walked round Melrose Abbey, the ruins glorious in the sunshine. The abbey church is still a splendid edifice; viewed from the south it is a fascinating collection of spires, buttresses and archways.

I left town and headed west. An hour later, at Tweedbank, I realised I had left my mobile phone at the abbey, so I took a bus back to Melrose. Outside the abbey I met an American locking up the tandem bike upon which he and his wife were touring the Borders. We got chatting and he asked me some questions about Scottish history. As we were walking uphill towards the centre of the village we were approached by a man asking if this was Meg. He went on to tell me he had enjoyed *Charlie, Meg and Me* so much that he had sent a copy to a friend in Australia.

My American companion asked, 'Is he an author?'

'Oh yes,' was the reply.

'Is he famous?'

'Oh yes,' the man responded, adding 'Meg's famous, aren't you Meg?'

Too late. The American chap shouted across the town square, which was milling with people: some standing chatting, others sitting outside at the café.

'Hey Karen. I've got a famous Scottish author over here,' he bellowed.

All over the busy square people turned to look. Heads were tipped forward and sunglasses pulled down just a touch, probably looking for Ian Rankin or JK Rowling. I wished the ground would open up and swallow me whole. It had been a long time since I had a brasser like that. I stood meekly professing my unfamousness to Brad, who

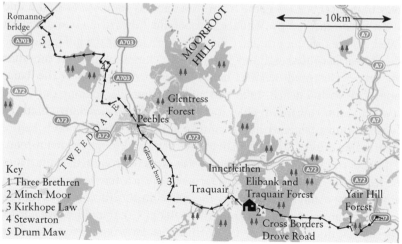

Cross-Borders Drove Road.

was having none of it.

Catching the bus back to Tweedbank, I resumed walking and headed towards Galashiels along the A7. At the academy I picked up the Southern Upland Way and on leaving the woods below Gala Hill I crossed high, green fields and came down by Fairnlee Farm. Yair Bridge took me to the south bank of the Tweed and I headed into a forestry plantation below the hills of the old royal hunting grounds of the Ettrick Forest. Following the path upwards I emerged, panting heavily and sweating profusely, onto a heather-clad ridge on the southern slopes of the Three Brethren. Without the shelter of the trees the wind was punishing, but I slogged on up to the summit and rested behind one of the three giant cairns which mark the meeting of three estates. I wasn't my usual perky self. I felt listless and drowsy, so an hour later, still amongst the hills, I took shelter behind a dyke from the raging wind and cooked up an early dinner. A piece of toilet paper flew past me and stuck to my knee. 'Dig a hole, ya bastards!' I screamed at nobody in particular.

The next hill, Brown Knowe, was the highest of the day at 523m. Descending only slightly, the path met up with the Minchmoor Road, a track with which Bruce himself would have been familiar. Historically, this high level road was the main route across southern Scotland and used by armies led by Wallace, Bruce and Edward I. At the Cheese Well, where offerings of dairy produce were left for the hill fairies, the road begins to descend and I found Minchmoor bothy set amongst the trees. This small wooden cabin has a porch built along the front, complete with a bench. Like 'old ma' I sat outside, looking down the Tweed Valley towards Peebles, only wishing I had a rocking chair.

I was up early and had a sunrise breakfast on the porch before continuing onwards to Traquair. At Kirkhouse, leaving the main road, I joined the Cross Borders Drove Road, a waymarked route from Yarrowford in the Borders to Harperrig, just a few kilometres from Edinburgh. Annually, between the 16th and 19th centuries, up to 100,000 cattle were driven from the trysts at Crieff and Falkirk across the border and all the way to Norfolk, for fattening, before the final journey to London. The drovers would have loved all the luxuries

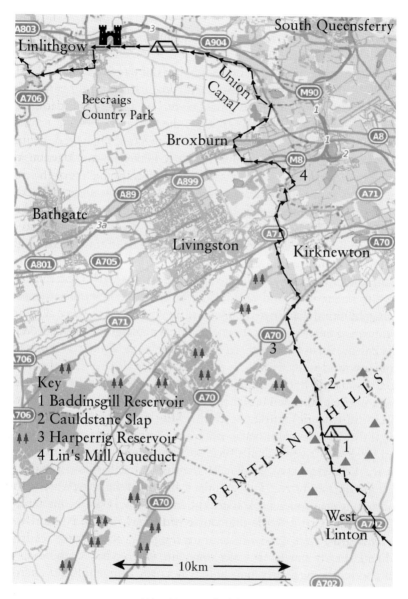

West Linton to Linlithgow.

I carried. These tough Highlanders slept beside their cattle wrapped in their plaid, and carried only some oatmeal, an onion or two and maybe a pistol for protection.

Following the Glass Burn through fields of pasture to heather-clad hills, I neared the summit of Birks Hill, where the path turns north to climb Kirkhope Law and stays high, traversing a long humpback ridge which flattens out near Peebles.

An ancient community, Peebles retains a vibrant High Street, where I was quite literally dragged into the Tweeddale Museum by a busker trying to drum up a crowd for a museum festival. In the forecourt I was introduced to the manager, a wood carver and some sheep but I had to get on, so I made my excuses, promising to bring the family back in the future. With 20km still to go and half the day already gone, I got the willies and rushed through the oldest part of town to catch the drove road once more. An ever changing series of paths brought me to Stewarton Farm and I charged on through the dark Cloich Forest, passing under, over and around the fallen trees. Emerging to open, rolling hillsides, the drove road wound its way round the base of Green Knowe and I followed the Fingland Burn, passing under Drum Maw and cutting across its northern flank, romping down to the hamlet of Romannobridge.

Crossing the A701, at one time the main road between Edinburgh and Dumfries, I headed into the historic village of West Linton, known as Linton Roderick (after the British King of Strathclyde) in Bruce's day. Edward I passed through the town, during his invasion of 1298 and Sir John Comyn, then overlord of the town, passed through on his way to a victorious battle with the English at Roslin in 1303. The meandering main street followed the direction of the Lyne Water north and I continued on a back road known as 'The Loan' to an ancient right of way that follows the course of an old Roman Road. I was really starting to feel the effects of my long day, but without realising it I had already started to make some inroads into the foothills of the Pentlands, a range of rolling hills which run from the southwest of Edinburgh to Upper Clydesdale. By evening I was well amongst them and camped on the lower slopes of Muckle Knock, just a stone's throw

Looking Back upon the Pentland Hills.

from the drove road above Baddinsgill Reservoir.

Some Highland cattle were waiting outside the tent to greet me as I arose and I considered the life of a drover as I continued through the hills – maybe this could be a future challenge, herding some cows from the Isle of Skye to Falkirk, the largest of all cattle markets. The route continued north, the last piece of remote walking of the journey. The summit of the path was at the Cauldstane Slap, an evocatively named pass between the hills of East Cairn and West Cairn – not so imaginatively named. The plain of the Firth of Forth opened before me, and it hit me that I was now on the last steps of this unforgettable journey. Apart from missing my other half and kids, I was comfortable with my nomadic lifestyle and I knew that the initial exuberance at the comforts of home would wear off within a day or two of crossing the threshold. Sitting in an office during the day, I would soon be longing for lost liberty.

It was a steady descent to Harperrig Reservoir where I joined up with the road network for a couple of hours until I reached the Union Canal at Lin's Mill aqueduct, between Ratho and Broxburn. I was sitting on a bench cooking up my lunch, watching small boats, passing paddlers and fishermen when a large canal barge, *The Pride of the Union*, came round the corner and pulled up alongside me. Inside, groups of people were sitting at nicely decorated tables, tucking into five star lunches, sipping wine and conversing with family and friends, while I'm sitting with nowhere to look but at them, eating my super noodles from a pan. Soon people were piling out and wandering across the 130m aqueduct which spans the River Almond 23m below.

Opened in 1822, the 32-mile Union Canal connects Edinburgh with Falkirk. On a warm, sunny afternoon, with nothing to worry about and Meg free to do as she pleased, I daydreamed my way along the towpath towards Linlithgow. On the way I met a suntanned couple who were walking from John o' Groats to Land's End – a 1,200-mile walk, which gazumped me. They were using the Scottish National Trail, developed by Cameron McNeish, to traverse Scotland, but were a bit fed up with canals. They had followed the Forth and Clyde Canal from Glasgow to Falkirk and had started out on the Union Canal, which they would be following into Edinburgh.

On the outskirts of the historic town of Linlithgow, I was given permission to camp in a field alongside the waterway. Although in decline all too soon after their construction – due to the advent of the railway – these rejuvenated canals are a great asset for walkers, runners, cyclists, sailors and paddlers, enabling them to travel across the Central Belt free of traffic and surrounded by serenity. I was ahead

The Union Canal at Linlithgow.

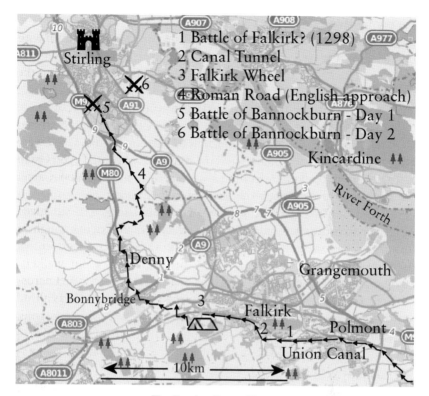

1 Battle of Falkirk? (1298)
2 Canal Tunnel
3 Falkirk Wheel
4 Roman Road (English approach)
5 Battle of Bannockburn - Day 1
6 Battle of Bannockburn - Day 2

The Road to Bannockburn.

of schedule and could afford to take my time when I walked into the town the next morning to visit Linlithgow Palace. The staff were delighted to meet Meg and they gave me the lowdown on the beautiful but roofless royal accommodation. In the courtyard, the impressive North Range filled my gaze: between two towers is a facade of five storeys, dominated by 32 windows, each with a carved triangular pediment. This building, when decorated and lit, was designed to create an impression of grandeur to visiting guests in the 17th century. Built from 1424 onwards, the palace was oft-times home for the Stuart Kings from James I onwards. It was the birthplace of both Mary Queen of Scots and her father, James V, who commissioned the elaborate fountain in the centre of the courtyard. Climbing up to the top of the corner tower, I met the palace manageress, all suited up, cleaning pigeon poop from the top of the staircase. I tried to justify my theory that some of the palace dated to Robert the Bruce's time or even that he got married in St Michael's Kirk next door. The manageress wasn't having any of it and I could tell she thought there was more poop coming from me than there was stuck on the concrete steps!

The palace was built upon the site of a timber peel (a place fortified by ditch, bank and palisade) which was surrounded by Linlithgow Loch. In 1313, a local man, William Bunnock, captured the peel in a way that inspired countless films – a haycart, supposedly bringing supplies, was driven inside the gates and abandoned, preventing the gates from closing and the drawbridge from rising. The attackers hidden within the cart jumped out to attack the peel's guards. Other Scots broke from cover to charge inside and help overpower the garrison.[31]

The taking of Linlithgow, along with Edinburgh, Roxburgh, Dirleton and many other castles, shows the peculiar predicament that was Lothian in the period 1306–14. Many of its chief men and castles were loyal to Edward II, and thus Robert the Bruce was minded to treat the area as he did the north of England: pay a ransom, or else have your lands destroyed. Local people were also harried by hostile castle garrisons and found themselves in a no-win situation. Anyway, by the time that Edward marched north in 1314, almost all the castles in Lothian had been recaptured. Edward would find no succour in Lothian as he marched north to Stirling.

Next to the palace is the beautiful St Michael's Church, with its iconic aluminium crown. The church was around in the time of Bruce, although it has been rebuilt a couple of times since. I had lunch nearby, sitting outside at the Strawberry Café, and continued through the town to find my way back to the canal. Crossing the Avon Gorge on the UK's second longest aqueduct was as dramatic as the 15km walk got, but it was enjoyable now to be walking in familiar territory, so close to home. Looking over to Hallglen, I saw the slopes which are topped with Callendar Woods. These slopes are one of the favoured locations for the Battle of Falkirk (1298). Wallace addressed his troops

The canal tunnel at Falkirk.

prior to the battle. 'I have brought you to the ring, now dance if you can'. Despite the Scots' schiltroms putting up a valiant defence against the English cavalry, Edward I used the devastating power of massed English and Welsh archers to break up the Scots ranks. It was a major defeat for Wallace and came all too soon after his great victory at Stirling Bridge the previous year. In Falkirk Old Parish Church is the grave of Sir John de Graham, Wallace's companion, who was killed at the battle. There is also a commemorative monument to the men of the Isle of Bute, none of whom returned home.

I passed through a 577m canal tunnel, once a long, dark and hazardous journey for pedestrians. A handrail and electric lighting have removed the peril, although that hadn't stopped me from getting a fright on a routine walk with the dog: the lights used to go out at 9pm and on one occasion Meg (leadless as usual) and I were walking through the tunnel in the pitch dark, rather than make a big detour, when a cyclist entered the tunnel at the opposite end. He reached us and was passing by when Meg got spooked, probably by his lamp, and jumped to the side; I heard a splash. I couldn't see anything but I knew there was no way she could climb out with the concrete towpath a good bit higher than the water level. The cyclist fled, and I was left in the dark once more. I lay on the path and put my arm in the water, searching around frantically. Finally, I got a hold of her and fished her out.

Three kilometres further along the canal bank is the outstanding Falkirk Wheel, which connects the Forth & Clyde and Union canals. Completed in 2002, this masterpiece of engineering, a unique rotating wheel lift, raises boats and barges 24 metres to allow them to sail between canals. The iconic structure has helped to give the town of Falkirk a positive and modern symbol which visitors can identify. The newly revealed Kelpies, 30m-high equine monuments made from stainless steel, are also sure to become a hit with tourists from around the world. They are the centrepiece of the Helix Project, a huge recreational area developed from reclaimed land.

On top of an old bing where the ground is slowly returning to its natural state I made my final camp, looking out over my home town. The next morning I was interviewed on Radio Scotland and sought some sympathy for my stupidity. I had stood on a tent peg to force it into hard ground and had only succeeded in piercing my shoe and bruising my foot. It looked like I would be hobbling over the finish line.

One of the many paths that crisscross the area led me to the Antonine Wall. Built by the Romans from AD 142 to protect the Empire from the northern tribes, it stretched 60km from Old Kilpatrick to Bo'ness, and is now a UNESCO World Heritage Site. The accompanying military road would have provided excellent east–west communications 1,700 years before the canals ever did. I do like this stretch of the wall at the site of Rough Castle Fort near Bonnybridge; walking along the ditch which was an extra defensive barrier in front of the 3m high turf wall allows the imagination to run amok. Nearby, pits have been uncovered, called 'Lilia'; these would have been concealed and contained pointed stakes to disrupt any attack.

With excitement starting to mount, I passed through the villages of Bonnybridge, Denny and finally Dunipace, where I stopped for a lovely Scottish breakfast at Café Luisa – this was turning into a triumphal progress rather than an exhausting end to a gruelling walk. At the West Plean crossroads I turned left to follow the old Roman road. Mighty Stirling Castle was straight ahead, beckoning me onwards, just as it would have done for Edward II in 1314. The English King was trying to save his father's last conquest in Scotland. Edward II must have been utterly appalled at how it had all gone so wrong since the death of his sire. His control of Scotland had collapsed entirely and other than Stirling, Bothwell and Berwick, almost all other significant Scottish fortresses were now in Bruce's hands. Few Scottish allies remained and it was due to the plea of the Lothian lords such as Patrick, Earl of Dunbar, and Sir Adam Gordon that Edward found himself in Scotland this year, determined to destroy the rising of Robert the Bruce, once and for all.

Barbour relates that Robert the Bruce was angry with his brother for having made a pact with the governor of Stirling Castle, Sir Philip Mowbray, in 1313, that if the fortress was not relieved by midsummer's day 1314 then it would be handed over to the Scots. This was a challenge that would bring Edward II to Scotland at the head of a powerful army, and gave the English monarch a whole year to prepare and recruit.

This timing is wrong:[32] Edward II was informed only at the end of May 1314 of the recently made pact between Edward Bruce and Sir Philip Mowbray and he was already planning an invasion of Scotland because it was Robert Bruce who had lit the touch-paper which would bring the English north. In October 1313, King Robert issued an ultimatum to Scots nobles who refused to accept his kingship – come into the King's peace within 12 months or lose your lands forever.[33] It was this ultimatum that forced a reaction: Edward II was convinced to defend the interests of his Scots and English subjects who had lost land and title during Bruce's reign. A month later, he set about gathering an army to protect their perceived rights and to defeat Robert the Bruce's rebellion (as he saw it!) once and for all. A massive army was summoned from the counties of England, Wales and Ireland. Edward's plans to invade were in full swing and in fact he was less than 80km from Scotland when Sir Philip Mowbray caught up with him and told him of his agreement.

Bruce would have known that he would elicit a reaction from Edward II by his declaration to the disinherited, and must have made plans. Firstly, by capturing the important royal castles of Roxburgh and Edinburgh, he would deny the English any secure bases for any Scottish campaign. Nor could any campaign objective of Edward II be to win them back – they were destroyed. I agree with some historians that Bruce, when he found out that the English were on the march, deliberately sought to draw Edward II to Stirling by intimidating the governor of Stirling Castle into making a deal. Having seen the equally powerful strongholds of Edinburgh and Roxburgh fall, Sir Philip Mowbray entered into a bargain to save his castle. The relief of Stirling Castle was in turn an offer that Edward II could not refuse, it was a powerful symbol of English royal authority, the scene of his father's last success in Scotland and an opportunity to force Bruce to fight.

Bruce could only win a battle against a superior English army if he was to bring into play all the aspects of guerrilla warfare that he had learned over the past eight years. He knew that he had no match for the heavy cavalry, long-range archers or superior numbers that an English army could field, so the effectiveness of these forces would have to be neutralised. Only by drawing the English to a battlefield of his choosing could Bruce hope to succeed.

For my own part, I had been to the battlefield at Loudon Hill where Bruce had disrupted a charge of English heavy cavalry with advantageous terrain and pits dug into the ground. At Huntly, he had hidden his forces on a hilltop and at the Pass of Brander he trapped his opponents. At Clatteringshaws he had deceived an English force into retreating and at Inverurie he had abandoned a strong defensive position to attack. The tactics used at the Battle of Bannockburn had been learned in a variety of locations across Scotland. I knew he was ready.

Bruce sought to control the forthcoming battle: by forcing the English to come to Stirling he could meet them on ground of his choosing – ground that had been prepared in advance with pits dug to obstruct cavalry. Terrain that suited the Scots, giving them the defensive advantage of hilly ground. Marshy, wooded territory would negate the power of archers and cavalry. By making the English come quickly in order to relieve the castle by midsummer's day, they would be tired. Keeping them away from the coast would prevent them linking up easily with their supply ships. Operating a scorched earth policy in Lothian ensured the army of Edward II would be hungry. Without royal castles to use as staging posts en route to Stirling, supplies and morale would be stretched even further.

Bruce, meanwhile, could train his army for the battle that he anticipated. The numbers are guesswork but may have been in the region of 6,000–8,000 men, including 500 light cavalry. The foot soldiers were trained to operate in schiltroms, tightly packed formations wielding long spears called pikes. These formations had initially succeeded at the Battle of Falkirk, but this time Bruce taught them to be mobile, rather than the static force they were under William Wallace – a vital tactic. The Scots would be properly rested and prepared, and highly motivated under the leadership of a proven winner.

When the day finally arrived and as the vanguard of the huge English army approached Stirling along the Roman road, Bruce's forces were hidden in the trees at the New Park, preventing the English from advancing any further. The English army would have been in the region of 15,000 men, including heavy cavalry and longbowmen, specialist forces unavailable to the Scots.

The first troops on the scene, the cavalry of Edward's vanguard, attacked the Scots' schiltroms but were rebuffed, and in a legendary incident, Bruce showed the martial skills which he had been developing his whole life. Mounted on an inferior palfrey, he was charged by an impatient English knight. Avoiding the lance of the onrushing Henry de Bohun with skilful manoeuvring of his nimble pony, he brought down his battleaxe upon the English knight's helmet, killing him instantly. A rash encounter which could have ended things there and then, had it gone awry for the King, instead resulted in a massive morale boost for the Scottish army. Next, Edward sent an outflanking force of cavalry around the Scots' position to relieve the castle. This was defeated by a schiltrom led by the Earl of Moray.

Possibly fearful of a surprise attack during the night, Edward II decided to send his army down to the Carse of Balquhiderock to camp on an area of low, marshy ground enclosed by both the Bannock and Pelstream Burns which would offer protection if Bruce tried any overnight shenanigans. The English infantry would have been exhausted and hungry after their forced march north, and the midges of the carse would have made for an uncomfortable evening as the army reflected on the events of day one. Worse was to follow for the beleaguered English army, because Edward's conventional thinking had led him into a trap of his own making!

Overnight, Bruce abandoned his positions defending the Roman road, with all the prepared defences. He turned his army a quarter turn to face east and the disciplined schiltroms led by trusted, experienced, battle-hardened lieutenants, advanced down upon the English camp, marching out of a strong defensive site that offered cover from archers, protection from cavalry and the advantage of higher slopes, onto an army twice as large as his own. Bruce was making a bold manoeuvre.

Early the following morning, the Scots emerged from the forest, lined up and ready to face the forces of Edward II. They advanced upon the surprised English who found themselves hemmed in within their defensive campsite and unable to deploy their archers or cavalry divisions properly. The massive size of their army worked against them and they were cut down mercilessly by the pike-wielding patriots. A company of archers did eventually manage to disentangle themselves from the melee and began to pour arrows down upon the Scots from the flank, but these were dispersed by Bruce's light cavalry, which he had held in reserve. The hand-to-hand fighting at the front line would have been grim and relentless: the Scots, scything and stabbing their way forward; the English defending desperately with no room either to manoeuvre or retreat.

The final act of the battle was the arrival on the scene of a band of

Scottish extras, the so called 'sma' folk' – men who had arrived too late to be incorporated within the schiltroms, as well as opportunists, camp followers and youths etc. The battle now turned into a rout as the English soldiers, seeing another Scottish force, sought to flee the field. Many would have been slaughtered or drowned as they attempted to cross the Bannockburn. A chance of escape would only have come to those who got past their own supply train, where many of the victorious Scottish soldiers would have stopped to take their rightful booty.

The exact location of the events of the Battle of Bannockburn has been subject to much debate over the past 100 years, but never more than during the run-up to the 700th anniversary of the battle. The sequence and locations that I have outlined were first proposed by General Sir Philip Christison in 1960[34] and have been corroborated recently by Dr Tony Pollard, Director of the Centre for Battlefield Archaeology, who has conducted two years of research into the battle while making *The Quest for Bannockburn*. There have been many theories on the exact location of the battle and the evidence collected for the BBC TV programme has helped to confirm the above sequence of events. My own small contribution was as one of the hundreds of volunteers who participated in digs organised by the National Trust for Scotland in 2012 and 2013. I dug up some medieval green glazed pottery from the carse area. On its own it proved nothing, but it helped to establish that there was activity in this marshy area.

Dr Pollard summarises the battle brilliantly: 'Bruce prepared for a Loudon Hill, and he got a Stirling Bridge.' This was the true genius of Robert the Bruce, his adaptability and his ability to change a plan that had been so meticulously prepared. With everything at stake that he had built since 1306, he made the most brilliant moves to win the battle. Having done a good bit of wargaming in my youth, I can relate to this tactical brilliance – I took a few hammerings from a superior general. Seeing the moves my opponent made, I thought I could have won with his army. We then switched sides, he took my forces, and I took his. He won again! He had the ability to think on the spot and change his plan accordingly, whereas I tried to copy the moves of the previous battle.

The other piece of genius, I believe, was leading Edward II into the trap that was Bannockburn. When Bruce discovered that Edward II was set on invading Scotland in 1314, he ensured that the English King came to his chosen battleground by tempting him with the bait of relieving Stirling Castle, the last conquest of his father. Bruce could thus bring all the stratagems of his guerrilla warfare campaigning to bear at Bannockburn.

After the battle, King Edward II escaped but many leading Englishmen did not. They were either slain on the field or captured by the Scots. The battle greatly enriched Bruce's treasury, as all the belongings of the huge army were captured. Equally valuable were the captives. The Earl of Hereford was exchanged for Bruce's Queen, his daughter and other females captured in 1306. Bishop Wishart was also returned home. Wishart had gone blind in captivity, but lived to know that Scotland's future looked to be assured in Bruce's hands.

Stirling Castle, swiftly followed by Bothwell Castle was handed over to the Scots. Berwick was the only strength of any note that remained under English control. The peace however, took longer to win than the war. Despite this victory, followed up by the subjugation of northern England, as well as an attempt to unseat the English dominion in Ireland, the English King was incredibly stubborn and refused to accept Robert Bruce, as King of Scots. In 1327, Edward's continuing unpopularity with his own nobles led to him being deposed and then murdered; he was replaced by his son Edward III. In the same year, the Scots completed yet another successful campaign in England, with Bruce threatening to annex the territory of Northumberland to the Scottish Crown. The new regime came scurrying to the negotiating table.

Bruce dictated the terms of the peace treaty, making six points that he demanded be agreed upon by Edward III's government. The main item was that Bruce and his heirs be recognised undisputed Kings of Scots and in no way beholden to the Kings of England. Bruce also proposed that his son marry Edward's sister and promised to pay £20,000 to make good for damages caused. The Treaty of Edinburgh was signed at Holyrood Abbey in 1328.

The most unlikely turnaround in fortunes was complete. A whole kingdom had been torn from the clutching grasp of England's Plantagenet rulers. Scotland's independence was won and Bruce had masterminded the most unlikely of triumphs. From the darkest days, hiding in the Trossachs and the most desperate of pursuits in the Galloway Hills, Bruce was now established monarch of a country that had been brought back from the brink of extinction.

Having followed Bruce from these terrible lows to ultimate highs, I appreciated the huge physical triumph this was, never mind the battles and the politics. His life and possibly Scotland's future as a nation hung in the balance in the first few years of his kingship. I hoped that my efforts had done justice to the memory of that achievement and within myself I felt I had paid my respects in my own way.

Still a little ahead of schedule, I took a final stop on my triumphal progress and hid out at the Bannockburn Inn for a couple of hours; I couldn't arrive at the Battlefield Heritage Centre before my welcoming party! Despite the vast array of celebratory drinks on offer, I restrained myself one final time and sat with a diet cola, realising it was all coming to an end. I had done it, I had walked a thousand miles, survived my tent and my cooking and had taken in a shedload of history along the way. I had learned a lot about Bruce, about Scotland and about myself.

My reception as I walked jauntily into the car park was arrayed not in a schiltrom, but standing in a line in front of the heritage centre. Family and friends with St Andrews crosses waving, embraces many and heartfelt. It was delightful to be welcomed so warmly and I felt on top of the world. Nicola

Meg having a well-earned drink at Bannockburn.

and the girls rushed up to meet me, Sophie and Kara momentarily forgetting their teenage reluctance. My youngest daughter Abbie's face was a picture of happiness as I picked her up for a cuddle and twirl. It was the perfect homecoming. Meg bounded around, sprinting between compassionate calls. Nine weeks ago she had gone for a walk and never came back – she must have wondered what the hell had happened. Now, with all the familiar faces greeting her, she knew she was home. I walked contentedly with Nicola and my welcome party to the newly renovated statue of a mounted, armoured Bruce; the frowning warrior king surveying his most famous victory.

Within the brand new Bannockburn Heritage Centre is a 3D battle experience and a 20-person wargame where I could practise my skills. On this occasion, I headed for a beer, sandwiches and cake, and to begin the long process of catching up with what had been going on in everyone else's lives these past weeks. For my own part, I told them I was happy, fit and more confident than ever before; ready to be a family man once again, but already with thoughts of how I could push myself just a little bit further next time.

Timeline

1274	July	Birth of Robert Bruce at Turnberry Castle, Ayrshire.
1286	March	Death of King Alexander III of Scotland leaving only an infant granddaughter in Norway as heir to the throne.
	April	Guardians appointed to rule realm.
1290	September	Death of the 'Maid of Norway' en route to Scotland.
1291	October	King Edward I of England is sought to select a King for Scotland.
1292	November	John Balliol is selected King of Scots from a list of claimants. He is crowned at Scone.
1296	March	Outbreak of hostilities between King John and King Edward. Berwick is captured and sacked.
	April	Scots defeated at the Battle of Dunbar.
	July	Abdication of King John. Scottish Kingship abolished.
	August	'Ragman's Roll' is collated at Berwick. Over 2,000 Scots signatories pledge homage to Edward I
1297	May	Wallace and Bruce begin, independently, to revolt against English rule.
	September	Andrew Murray and Wallace defeat an English army at Stirling Bridge. Murray is badly injured; Wallace is appointed Guardian of Scotland.
1298	July	Edward I defeats Scots army led by Wallace at Battle of Falkirk. Wallace resigns Guardianship. John Comyn and Robert Bruce appointed Guardians of Scotland.
1300	May	Bruce resigns as Guardian.
1302	February	Bruce submits to Edward I and marries Elizabeth de Burgh.
1304	February	John Comyn submits to Edward I.

1305	August	Wallace captured and executed.
1306	February	Bruce stabs John Comyn at Greyfriars Kirk, Dumfries.
	March	Bruce is crowned King Robert I at Scone, Perthshire.
	June	The new King is defeated at Battle of Methven
	August	Robert's forces are ambushed at Dalrigh. Thereafter the King is a fugitive.
	September	King Robert I flees mainland Scotland.
1306–7	Winter	Bruce recruits an army, possibly from the Western Isles and northern Ireland.
1307	February	King Robert returns to Turnberry, Ayrshire.
	April	A victory for Bruce at Glen Trool.
	May	Another victory for the Scots at the Battle of Loudon Hill.
	July	Death of King Edward I of England.
	September	Bruce gathers his supporters and heads north.
	October	Inverlochy Castle is captured.
	December	Skirmish at Slioch near Huntly between the forces of the King and Comyn.
1308	May	Comyns defeated by Bruce at Battle of Inverurie
	July	Aberdeen Castle captured.
	August	The MacDougalls defeated by the King at the Pass of Brander.
	October	At Auldearn Castle, the Earl of Ross comes into the King's peace.
	December	Forfar Castle captured and destroyed.
1309	March	Parliament is held at St Andrews Cathedral.
1310	September	Edward II of England invades Scotland.
1312	August	The Scots raid the north of England.
1313	January	Perth captured by Bruce.
1314	February	James Douglas captures Roxburgh Castle.
	March	Edinburgh Castle captured by Thomas Randolph
	June	Battle of Bannockburn.
1315	May	The Scots invade Ireland, led by Edward Bruce.
1316	May	Edward Bruce is crowned King of Ireland.
1317	January	Robert Bruce travels to Ireland in support of his brother.

1318	April	Randolph and Douglas capture Berwick.
	October	Death of Edward Bruce.
1320	April	Declaration of Arbroath.
1322	August	Edward II invades Scotland.
1322	October	Bruce invades England and defeats English at Battle of Old Byland.
1324	January	Bruce recognised as King of Scots by papacy.
1327	January	King Edward II of England is deposed.
	February	Scots attack Norham Castle.
	June–August	James Douglas and Thomas Randolph raid. Durham and confront newly crowned Edward III.
	September	Bruce invades Northumberland forcing English to begin peace negotiations.
1328	March	Treaty of Edinburgh recognises Bruce as Independent King of Scots.
	July	Bruce's son David marries English Princess Joan of the Tower.
1329	June	Death of Robert Bruce at his manor in Cardross.
1330	August	Death of James Douglas, protector of the King's heart, at the Battle of Teba.